DATE DUE

CANADIAN OCCASIONS

CANADIAN OCCASIONS

ADDRESSES

BY

JOHN BUCHAN
(LORD TWEEDSMUIR)

Essay Index Reprint Series

BOOKS FOR LIBRARIES PRESS
FREEPORT, NEW YORK

First Published 1940
Reprinted 1969

STANDARD BOOK NUMBER:
8369-1275-6

LIBRARY OF CONGRESS CATALOG CARD NUMBER:
70-90618

PRINTED IN THE UNITED STATES OF AMERICA

CONTENTS

I. Ave

3

VIII. The Learned Professions

IX. Literature

I

AVE

AVE[1]

A S I look round this audience I see some of my former
colleagues in British politics, and, looking at them
I feel that this occasion, for me, is in the nature of a
farewell to many cherished activities. I detect in their
eyes an obituary solemnity. But when I look at others,
my Canadian friends—many of them of old standing—
I realise that to-night is also the inauguration for me of
something new—a message of God-speed from those
who know Canada to one who has little knowledge but
abundant good will.

Let me say at once that I rejoice at the opportunity
which has been given me. I have seen the prowess of
Canadians in two wars. I have known them in sport,
in business and in scholarship. I have seen enough of
the beauty of their land to make me long to see more.
If in any way, however humble, I can serve Canada
and her people, I shall consider that my life has not
been wasted.

I am an historian, and therefore a lover of old things,
and I am going to a country which is long-descended.
I shall be the thirty-fifth Governor-General, if you
count only from the conquest of Canada by Britain.
But if you count from its first settlement by the
gentlemen-adventurers of France, I shall be the fifty-
first. There are not many nations which can boast of a
more tempestuous and heroic youth. For a century
there were wars between French and English, between
white man and red man. For three hundred years there

[1]*Canada Club Dinner. London. 27th May, 1935.*

9

has been a war which is not yet concluded—the war of man against the wilds. Canada is an old country, though her history is short compared with Britain's. But in one sense she is Britain's senior. Constitutionally all the autonomous units of the Empire are to-day equal sovereign States under one King. That is to say, they are Dominions: and of these Dominions Canada is the oldest and Britain is the youngest.

I have no authority to speak of Canada to-night, as many of you have, for my knowledge of her is still slight. And I am not going to conceal my ignorance by repeating platitudes which can be found in any reference book—about what she has done in the past in a hundred spheres of activity, or about what she has the power and the intention to do in the future. But, I have long been a student of public affairs, and, if I may, I should like to say one word about the kind of ultimate problem which she has to face in common with all the world.

The economic tempest of recent years has smitten every land impartially, the new as well as the old. Now, we old countries have for a long time had to husband our resources and think hard about our future. We have suffered so many set-backs that we have become skilled in the technique of disaster. But to the younger nations the problem used to be simple. Push the frontier a little further back—so ran the answer—strike out new lines, develop new wealth; the wealth is there; it only wants hard work and enterprise to win it. The situation is changed to-day. In a very real sense there are no frontiers left on the physical map. They must be sought in the world of the mind and the spirit. A country may have immense undeveloped material resources, but these are not wealth which can be easily and confidently realised; they do not become wealth until and unless they can be related to the demands and the uses of the rest of the world. That is to say, for a country to advance or even to keep its position there is needed a sustained effort of intelligent thought, a continuous adjustment and construction. A fresh economic and social mechanism has to be created, and the new countries are in this difficulty as compared to the older ones—they have less experience of this kind of creation, and they have to improvise in a brief time a machinery which the old lands may have already constructed at their leisure.

That is the problem of the United States to-day. It is in large measure Canada's problem. It is in some sense the problem of every people, and its successful solution depends upon how far a nation brings to the task a disciplined spirit, a stout heart and a clear head. I have no doubt as to how Canada will face it. She starts with immense advantages. She has the vitality and the adaptability of a young nation. Can we forget what happened twenty years ago when, for a wholly novel type of war, she produced an army which had no superiors and few equals on any front? That army was the spear-point, you remember, in the first great step in the Allied advance to victory, the Battle of Amiens on August 8th, 1918, and just because Canada's reputation was so tremendous, it was necessary to mislead the enemy by pretending, by the use of dummy soldiers, that the Canadians were in a part of the line fifty miles away. Can you imagine a higher compliment? Can you conceive a greater proof of national vitality?

But if Canada has the vigour of youth, she has also the balance and the just perspective of maturity. She is an integrated nation, united long ago by her own act, and with her unity riveted and compacted by partnership in the enterprises of peace and the sacrifices of war. And from Britain and France she draws the same tradition—that great Mediterranean tradition of Greece and Rome, which I believe to be the basis of civilisation. She is no rootless people, deriving a fickle inspiration from transient fashions, but a nation broad-based upon the central culture of mankind. She has her own proud heritage and she is loyal to it, for the first of virtues in a people or an individual is loyalty to what they know and love. That I hope and believe is the prime quality of our Empire and of all its constituent parts.

Canada has completed her pioneering stage, her romantic adolescence. Yes, but she has still pioneering before her as difficult as any in the past, and adventures not less fateful. The world to-day is one vast laboratory of new experiments. Every problem is changing and requires a fresh analysis. The quality of a nation will be tested by its power of facing novel situations with clear eyes and steady nerves. The peril—and, make no mistake, there is a very real peril—the peril for the world lies in a light-headedness which is content to be flippant and cynical and destructive, and a timidity which makes men forget their manhood and rush in panic to any shelter.

The courage to construct, the insistence that every man shall be able to stand on his own feet and be the master of his soul—these things mean the defence of true democracy. For it is democracy, the very essence of our political faith, that is at issue. The modern State is such a complex affair that there are many people who have come to believe that it cannot be administered on the old line of personal freedom. They say that freedom is inconsistent with efficiency. We have seen proud nations lose heart and surrender themselves to a dictator.

It is for us to show a better way, to prove to the world that civilisation has twin foundations, and that, if one of them is law, the other is liberty.

I have said that the task before Canada to-day is more fateful and more vital than that struggle by which she first came into being. Then she was fighting for her bare existence. Now she is assisting to preserve our hard-won civilisation. She has to win back prosperity for herself, and in so doing she has to help to stabilise the world. For I firmly believe that the task of restoring a slightly lunatic world to sanity, of safeguarding the bulwarks of liberty and civilisation, must fall mainly upon the British peoples. It is a task which might well fire any patriotic spirit—to be a trustee and defender of profound truths which the foolish have forgotten.

In this task she is not alone, but moving and working within the great framework of the Empire. That Empire to-day, as we all know, is an executive partnership which involves the pooling of interests and ideas and the linking together of energies. Its prestige has never been higher. The words which Burke used 150 years ago are even truer to-day: "We are set on a conspicuous stage and all the world marks our demeanour." First of all we present an example of disciplined freedom, ordered liberty. In the second place we present an example of nations holding fast to their old traditions, but facing the future with clear and candid eyes— at once rational revolutionaries and rational conservatives. And lastly we are a living proof that peoples can dwell together in unity and peace, for have we not made in the Empire a league of nations of our own, and insured that over a great part of the earth's surface there can never be war?

For three hundred years Canada's story has been

that of the slow conquest of the wilds. To-day she is
still the pioneer, but a pioneer in the overthrowing of a
more dangerous barbarism, in driving a path through a
more tangled wilderness, the wilderness of human fears
and human perversities. It is a great task—I cannot
imagine a greater. She has behind her a famous
tradition, to the making of which Britain and France
have given of their best. If she brings to the task that
ancient, proud and indomitable spirit then her success
is as certain as the rising of the sun.

II

GENIUS LOCI

THE WESTERN MIND[1]

I UNDERSTAND that it is my duty this afternoon to deliver to you a short address. It occurs to me that I might say something pertinent to the special position of McGill in this great city of Montreal.

Montreal is something more than the largest Canadian city; it is one of the most historic. Much history has been made around its walls. It is the chief city of a province which exhibits a phenomenon, happily common in our Empire, the friendly union of two races. Like all Scotsmen, I have an hereditary affection for France. Do you remember, in Stevenson's novel *Catriona*, how, at a critical moment in the adventures of David Balfour and Alan Breck, Alan turns to David and says, "They are a real bonny folk, the French nation"? I have always subscribed to Alan's view. It seems to me that one of the chief safeguards for the future of the world must be a close understanding between the British Empire and the Republic of France. Just before I left England we entertained Marshal Pétain, and he said one thing which impressed me. He said that he would like to see the day when a young Englishman naturally finished his education in France, and a young Frenchman naturally completed his training in Britain. You are fortunate here in Canada, where this admirable curriculum can be more or less achieved within the boundaries of your own country.

But I am not going to talk to you about the political aspects of that friendship. I would rather turn your

[1]*McGill University. Montreal. 23rd November, 1935.*

17

mind for a few minutes to the tradition of which, in a
special degree, Britain and France are the guardians in
the Old World, and of which, it seems to me, you in
Canada, where the two strains are united, should be the
special guardians in the New World. I call that tradition the Mediterranean tradition, which descends from
Greece and Rome, and therefore carries with it the
whole classical culture, and which, in the Middle Ages,
was enlarged and adapted by the Christian Church,
and amplified by bequests from the Northern peoples.
I will not attempt to trace its historical sequence.
Suffice it to say that on it are based the thought and
the philosophy, the art and the letters, the ethics and
religion of the modern world. It is the foundation of
civilisation, as we understand it. If I tried to describe
it in one word, I should take the Latin word *humanitas*.
It represents in the widest sense the humanities, the
accumulated harvest of the ages, the fine flower of a
long discipline of thought. It is the Western mind.

What are the characteristics of this Western mind, of
which the tap-root is the great Mediterranean tradition?
Let me suggest a few.

In the first place I think we may say that it is, in the
honourable sense of the term, worldly. It is pre-
eminently interested in the world which is governed by
the categories of space and time. In its outlook on
politics it is wholesomely secular. Therefore it can
never be put for long under any kind of theocracy.
Again and again, in the last thousand years of our
history, a theocracy has been tried. The story of the
early Middle Ages is the story of a bitter strife between
Church and State for a sovereignty which was partly a
secular sovereignty. A theocracy was set up by Calvin
in Geneva, but even in a single city it did not last long.

The same thing was tried in seventeenth century Scotland, and failed disastrously. The Western mind is determined that temporal things shall never be in the hands of the men whose business is with eternal things.

In the second place the Western mind has a strong bias towards a reasonable individualism. It insists on regarding human beings as individuals as well as units of society. It always finds some difficulty in the mystic idealisation of the State as a thing with rights far transcending those of its citizens. In the last resort it regards the *person* as what matters. Therefore it insists on a high degree of personal freedom. It believes that we are men and women, and not animals living in a hive or an ant-hill.

In the third place it is not very tolerant of abstractions. It likes concrete things and ideas which can be given a visible and tangible expression. It has its own poetry, of course, but it always returns to practical realities. It can never be captivated for very long by a bare theory, a mere idea. It may talk grandly about liberty and the rights of humanity, but, when it comes to fight, it will always be in order to get rid of some concrete abuse, or to establish some personal franchise. Therefore the State, as an abstraction, will not mean very much to it. Its affections are dedicated to a people or to a country—concrete things which anyone can understand.

Again, the Western mind has in a high degree an aptitude for discipline. It is always ready to accept leadership and to give loyal obedience. It is uncomfortable in a slack society, and whenever there has been a breakdown in institutions it has always looked about for some leader to restore discipline, and has sometimes given him a blind allegiance.

Again, it is interpenetrated with what may be called humour, a sense of proportion. It has that best of all gifts, the power of standing back occasionally and laughing at itself. It is perfectly capable of rhetoric, but it rarely carries rhetoric too far, for a wholesome and humorous realism creeps in. If it is given too much discipline its attitude will be that of the Highland crofter, who refused an extension of his holding, which involved keeping some thirty or forty official commandments, on the ground that he could get the whole of the Kingdom of Heaven by keeping ten! It puts an end to false heroics by a homely matter-of-factness, and it has an uncommon gift for pricking bubbles. Voltaire and Dr. Johnson were very different people, but they had the same antiseptic quality in their minds, and I think you will find this gift always present in the national genius of both Britain and France. Let me take a few parallels. In the seventeenth century you had Dryden and Molière; in the eighteenth Dr. Johnson and Voltaire; in the nineteenth, out of many, I should select George Meredith and Anatole France; and to-day, when we have few creative writers, but many good critics, I would instance Virginia Woolf and André Maurois. Neither race is inclined to a foolish extravagance. You remember the story of Dr. Jowett, the celebrated Master of Balliol. "Master," an earnest young man once asked him, "do you think a good man could be happy on the rack?" "Well," was the answer, "perhaps a very good man—on a very bad rack!"

Again, the Western mind has an acute sense of history. Its roots are deep down in the past. It realises that every problem is long-descended, and that, in Sir Walter Raleigh's words, "the councils to which Time is not called, Time will not ratify." It knows that society is a complex thing, the result of a slow growth, and no mere artificial machine. It holds that things die and must be cleared out of the road, that institutions and forms and dogmas lose the stuff of life and must be scrapped. But it also realises that in this world we cannot wipe the slate clean and write a new gospel on a virgin surface. It knows that true progress must be an organic thing, like the growth of a tree; that, if our building is to endure, we must make use of the old foundations, for otherwise we shall have a jerry-built erection which will presently fall about our ears.

Lastly, the Western mind is based upon the Christian ethics. I wish I could say, the Christian spirit. At the back of all its creeds is the acceptance, in the broadest sense, of the moral code of Christianity. It has often been unfaithful to it, but it knows that it has sinned against the light, and it has always returned to it. It is not capable, for example, of the solemn anarchy of a man like Nietzsche, who repudiated the whole of that moral code, or of those strange people in Germany to-day who follow the cult of Thor and Odin and the gospel of naked force. There is another point to notice, too. The Western mind believes in a reasonable degree of dogma and definition. It is not prepared to blur the outlines. It realises that life must be lived according to rules, and that though rules must be revised, some rules there must be, if civilisation is to continue. There is always a homely good sense in its idealism. It is a little suspicious of high-flying, transcendental creeds and a slack-lipped charity, for it believes that they may as easily have their roots in moral and intellectual slovenliness as in divine wisdom, and that the qualities which may characterise the saint are just as likely to be an attribute of the mollusc.

I suggest these characteristics to you as a step towards the definition and understanding of that great tradition which is the heritage of the English and French peoples. It is the basis of our politics; it is the basis of our art; it is the basis of our thought; and it is the basis of our conduct. To-day it has many critics. Because it involves discipline, it offends the natural rebel. Because it is based upon history, it is anti-pathetic to the *déracinés*, the rootless folk, who have no links with the past. Because it has balance and poise it is no creed for the neurotic. Because it is rich in spiritual ideals, it is no creed for the materialist. Because it is the faith of free men, it can never be a creed for the slavish and the timid. I have called it the central culture of civilisation, and I believe that is a true description. There are other cultures in the world, each with its own value for its own people. On them I pass no criticism, except to say that they are not ours, and that they do not mix well with ours. There is a good deal of anarchy in our art and letters to-day, caused by permitting alien elements—Slav, Mongol, Negroid—to intrude into a sphere in which they have no place. These elements have their value, no doubt, but that value is not for us, and I do not believe that we shall have again great poets, great artists, or great thinkers, except by a return to the tradition which in the past has produced the first order of genius, and whose inspiration is not exhausted.

As I have said, because of our happy race combination, Canada seems to me to be, in the New World, in a special degree the trustee of this tradition. One of the great germinal minds of the modern world was the Frenchman Voltaire, and no man ever guarded more vigilantly that freedom of spirit which is an essential part of it. Do you remember what he wrote in Chapter 23 of *Candide* about this country of yours:—"Vous savez que ces deux nations sont en guerre pour quelques arpents de neige, et qu'elles depensent pour cette belle guerre beaucoup plus que tout le Canada ne vaut." A few acres of snow! That is a remarkable instance of how bad a prophet a great man can be. I should like to think that these words in *Candide* will increasingly become one of the supreme examples of the irony of history, and that this Canada, of which Voltaire spoke so lightly, will be one of the principal wardens of the faith which, with all his imperfections, lay close to his heart.

Let my last word to you be that of John Ruskin, a writer a little neglected to-day, but one who was both a poet and a seer; "We are rich in an inheritance of honour bequeathed to us through a thousand years of noble history, which it should be our daily thirst to increase with splendid avarice."

THE GATE OF THE PACIFIC[1]

I HAVE the privilege of paying my first visit to you at an historic moment. In these weeks, when you have been celebrating your Jubilee, you have heard much about the fifty years behind you, during which Vancouver rose from a clearing in the forest to be the third city of Canada, and one of the most beautiful cities in the world. I remember that Mr. Kipling, who had travelled in most parts of the globe, once told me that he had found many places that he admired and some that he loved; but that he had discovered only one earthly paradise, and that was in British Columbia. I am a newcomer who has only had his first glimpse of you, but I can see no reason to differ from that verdict. You have created a wonderful metropolis, with the noblest natural background in the world.

To-day we are especially concerned with that great effort of faith and foresight, the railway which links you with the Atlantic. Fifty years ago I understand that the first trans-continental train had not yet reached you; you were an incorporated city before you were the end of steel. You had still to pass through the trial of the Great Fire. But a year later the railway was completed. To-day we take that miracle for granted, and familiarity has dulled our perception of the marvels of the achievement. For in sober truth the building of the Canadian Pacific was a miracle: it was an effort of faith which literally moved mountains. It gave the lie to the narrow economic interpretation of history. Canada's natural outlet lay to the south. She

[1]*Vancouver Jubilee Exhibition. August, 1936.*

24

chose, for a far-sighted political ideal, to make her development move westward, and thereby constituted herself in the fullest sense a great people with two oceans to serve her needs. She had long been a nation; but now she had an ample territory and a strategic and economic completeness.

No doubt Canada has much to do before she integrates her resources; like all the world, she has her urgent social and political questions; but I firmly believe that every problem is soluble, that every difficulty is temporary and remediable. I come to you with fresh eyes and, I hope, an open mind, but I am very certain that no Canadian is prouder of his country than I am, or believes more devoutly in her future.

In the destiny of Canada Vancouver must play a vital—I had almost said a dominant—part. For she is the window out of which Canada looks towards the East. She is the gateway to the Pacific. For forty-five years ocean-going steamers have sailed west from her quays. To-day fifty-five deep-sea lines use her harbour. She clears annually twelve million tons of shipping. She is the chief winter grain port of the world. It is not for me to forecast the future, but it is very clear that the East and the Pacific must play a major part in international affairs. It may well be that Vancouver will become the strategic vantage point in the economy of Canada and of the Empire. You are prepared for anything that fate may bring you, for you have a province whose riches have been scarcely tapped, a noble city and a strong and self-confident people. I am certain that when, fifty years hence, you celebrate your centenary you will look back upon even your present distinguished position as no more than the day of small things.

The Iceland Colony[1]

I WISH I could address you in your own ancient language. Long ago when I was a very young man I fell in love with the Icelandic Sagas, and I learned enough Icelandic to read them with some difficulty in the original. Alas! since then I have forgotten what little of the language I knew. But I have always been deeply interested in your race. The Scandinavian peoples are the close kinsfolk of the British. In my own country of Scotland there is a great deal of Norse blood. The Buchan region of Aberdeenshire, from which I take my name, was settled by Norsemen, for there the Vikings used to land to salt down the wild cattle for victuals on their long voyages. My own family is Norse in origin. I have travelled a good deal in Norway and the Northern Islands, and I have sailed the Northern Seas. Your race a thousand years ago were the great explorers of the world. When Britain was a jumble of tribes who never ventured beyond their own shores, your race had gone east to Constantinople and to Russia, and, first of all peoples, had landed on American soil. You have never lost that high tradition of enterprise and hardihood.

I have just been reading two interesting documents. One is the address of the Icelandic Society at Winnipeg, delivered fifty years ago to Sir John Macdonald, the Prime Minister of Canada, in which you asked for a greater encouragement of Icelandic settlement. The other is a speech of my predecessor, Lord Dufferin, ten

[1]*Gimli, Manitoba. September, 1936.*

years before to this very Settlement, in which he reminded you of your great traditions and wished you good fortune. I am glad to think that since these days your numbers have increased and your people are now a vital part of the Canadian nation. I wish we had more of you, for wherever I go in Canada I find the highest praise for the Scandinavian element. You have become in the fullest sense good Canadians, and have shared in all the enterprises and struggles of this new nation, and at the same time I rejoice to think that you have never forgotten the traditions of your homeland. That is the way in which a strong people is made—by accepting willingly the duties and loyalties of your adopted country, but also by bringing your own native traditions as a contribution to the making of Canada.

Sixty years ago Lord Dufferin remarked on the devotion which you retained for your Icelandic culture. It is a very great culture, and it contains some of the noblest literature ever produced by mortal men. Far up in that lonely Iceland, girt by stormy seas, you developed a mode of life which, for simple hardihood and manly independence, has not often been paralleled in history. And you have produced great literature. For myself I put the Icelandic Sagas among the chief works of the human genius.

There are two elements in your tradition, as reflected in the Sagas, on which I should like to say one word, for I hope that their spirit will never be forgotten. One is the belief in the reign of law. Everywhere in the Sagas you find that insisted upon. The old Icelanders were not only great warriors and adventurers, but they were acute lawyers and mighty jurists. Now, in these modern days, when in so many parts of the world there is a danger of the breakdown of law, that spirit seems

28 CANADIAN OCCASIONS

to me to be of the highest value. There can be no civilisation, no peace, unless the law of the community is made supreme over individual passions and interests.

The second element in the Saga tradition is still greater. As I see it, it is the belief that truth and righteousness must be followed for their own sake, quite independent of any material rewards. Consider what was the old Icelandic creed. Odin was the first of the gods, the personification of all manly virtues. But in their strange belief some day Odin was destined to be defeated; some day the powers of evil would triumph and Odin and his bright company would disappear into the dark. Yes, but that did not weaken the prestige of Odin, even though some day he was destined to fall. It was better to fall with Odin than to survive with the powers of evil.

That is the only true and manly morality. In these days when everyone is inclined to ask, in doing his duty, what he is going to get out of it, that noble spirit of un-self-regarding devotion is the true corrective. It was the creed of your forefathers. It is the creed of Christianity. It is the only creed which can put salt and iron and vigour into human life.

ISLAND MAGIC[1]

I AM glad to have at last reached this delectable island. I had hoped to come here more than a year ago, but circumstances prevented me. I know that you realise that my delay was not caused by any disrespect to one of the most interesting of all the Provinces of Canada. Wherever I go in the Dominion I meet your sons, generally in posts of high importance, and I have always been deeply impressed with their passionate affection for the place of their origin.

What is there about an island that makes its inhabitants regard it with peculiar pride? At the other end of Canada there is also an island, the island of Vancouver, where I have found a like pride and affection. It is the same all over the world. You remember the story of the minister in the little island of Cumbrae in the Firth of Clyde, who used to pray on Sunday for a blessing upon the Great and Little Cumbrae and upon the "adjacent islands of Great Britain and Ireland." That is the proper spirit. We British are an island people and it is to an island that our hearts return.

It has always been so in history from the time of the ancient Greeks, who placed their earthly Paradise not on any mainland, but in what they called the Fortunate Islands, somewhere out in the western ocean. It was from the island of Delos that the god Apollo sprang, and the little barren island of Ithaca was the home of the great Ulysses. From the tiny island of Iona Christianity came to Scotland. In one of the finest and

[1]*Charlottetown, Prince Edward Island. September, 1937.*

most poignant songs of exile ever written, the *Canadian Boat Song*, the heart of the wanderer does not turn back to any valley on the Scottish mainland. It is the "lone shieling on the misty island" of which he is thinking. It is the same throughout literature. In the Middle Ages romance centred in the mysterious islands of the western sea. It was on an island that Robinson Crusoe made his home. It was on Robert Louis Stevenson's "Treasure Island" that Jim Hawkins met his adventures.

What is it that gives an island this special charm for the heart of man? I think the main reason is that an island has its clear physical limits, and the mind is able to grasp it and make a picture of it as a whole. Our imagination may be kindled by big things—the far-stretching magnitude of the British Empire, or the vastness of the Dominion of Canada. But it is on little things that our affections lay hold. Cast back your memories to your childhood, and I think you will find that it is some modest-sized place that lingers most in your recollection, the wood where you played, a corner of the sea-shore, the little stream where you caught trout, the field which you regarded as your special property, the bit of the garden at home which was your own special garden. As we grow older our interests are enlarged, but our most idiomatic love is reserved for a village or a parish, what Edmund Burke, in a famous phrase, called "the little platoon in which we were reared." That is the fixed point from which we adjust ourselves to the rest of the world. Let me tell you a story which has the merit of being true. There is a parish in Scotland under the knees of the Grampians, called Rothiemurchus. A friend of mine was visiting some wounded soldiers returned from Mesopotamia, and she asked one man where he got his wound. His answer was "Weel, mem, it was about twa miles on the Rothiemurchus side of Bagdad." For that soldier the world was a simple place, for however far he wandered he could always link it up with his home. There is a profound parable in the saying. No experience will be too novel, and no place too strange if we can link it up with what we already know and love.

I do not think you can exaggerate the value of this local patriotism. The man who has it is at home in the world, for he has his roots deep down in his native soil. But to-night I want to put to you the other side of the matter. If it is essential to have the patriotism of the small unit, it is no less important to have the patriotism of the bigger unit. We begin with a loyalty to little things, a loyalty we should never relinquish—to our village, our parish, our home, our first school. But as we grow older it is important that we should acquire also wider loyalties—our college, our profession, our province, our nation, our fellow men. There is nothing inconsistent between a local patriotism and a patriotism of humanity. Indeed, I think the second is impossible without the first. There is no value in a thin international sentiment which professes an affection for humanity at large and shows no affection for the humanity immediately around us. The wider loyalty can only exist if the smaller loyalty is strong and deep. But there is need of the wider loyalty. Napoleon said very truly that Providence was on the side of the bigger battalions in war, and Providence is on the side, I think, of the bigger social battalions in the world to-day. In our complex modern life a large-scale organisation is essential if we are to get the best out of civilisation.

You of Prince Edward Island, like all strong peoples, represent a mixture of races. You have among you, I understand, a good many countrymen of my own. Now I am very chary about exaggerating the merits of Scotsmen, for we are only too prone to blow our own trumpet. We have plenty of faults—how many only a Scotsman knows! But we have one quality, I think, which can be praised without qualification. We have a gift of uniting the narrower and the wider patriotisms. We are scattered all over the globe, and wherever we go I think we become good citizens of our new home. Everywhere in the British Commonwealth, and in many lands which are not British, you will find Scotsmen taking a vigorous and loyal part in the national life. But at the same time we never forget the rock whence we were hewn and the pit whence we were digged. I find families of Scottish blood, which have been for generations away from Scotland, still retaining a lively affection for, and a lively interest in, their little country of origin.

That is as it should be, for a man can never have too many loyalties. Therefore I want to see in the citizens of Canada a strong and continuing love of the district to which they belong, but at the same time a strong and continuing interest in the Dominion of which they are a part, the whole Canadian nation.

A Governor-General is in a unique position, for it is his duty to get to know the whole of Canada and all the varieties of her people. This summer I had a trip of more than ten thousand miles, which took me in the tracks of Sir Alexander Mackenzie's journey to the Arctic Ocean, and over all the Northern territories, and also by Mackenzie's trail to the Pacific. In my two years of residence here I have already had the privilege

of visiting most parts of the different Provinces. I am
filled with admiration for what has already been done,
and with wonder and delight at the possibilities of the
future. You have a tremendous country, which I believe is destined to be one of the greatest nations in
the world.

So I want to make Canadians prouder of Canada—of
all Canada. You will only achieve your destiny if, in
addition to your strong love of your home, you have
also a pride and affection for the whole Dominion, a
loyalty to the vast territories which it is your business
to shape to the purposes of civilisation. I want the
older Canada, with its ancient and virile traditions, to
realise that these traditions must be not merely proud
memories, but an incentive to the shaping of the new
Canada, a summons to a high duty and a mighty task.
A famous English statesman once talked of calling in
the New World to redress the balance of the Old. The
duty before Canada and the duty before our British
Commonwealth of Nations is to use both Old and New
to provide for our people an ampler life.

Canada's Heritage[1]

I AM very glad to be with you to-day and to testify to my appreciation of the work you are doing and the immense importance of the problem which you are facing. The Canadian Forestry Association has now been in existence for forty years. It has done much to abolish the apathy towards the question of the last generation. It has done an immense amount of good educational work; it has forced the question of forest conservation upon the attention of Canada, so that it has become a matter of major public interest. I most warmly congratulate you upon your record of vital and unselfish public service.

I have now for four and a half years been going up and down the length and breadth of Canada, and I am lost in wonder at the magnitude of our assets. One of the greatest of these is our forests, the like of which you cannot parallel on the globe. Some of our assets are wasting assets, like our minerals, though it will be centuries, I believe, before we exhaust the riches of the Laurentian Shield. But our forests need not be a wasting asset. The beneficent renewing power of Nature brings a steady replacement to the vegetable world, that world on which all life, human and animal, is parasitic. Our forest wealth will only decline if we spend our capital unwisely. The richest man in the world would become a pauper if he squandered his capital without replacement.

In my young days in Scotland we suddenly woke to

[1]*Canadian Forestry Association. Montreal. 2nd February, 1940.*

the fact that we were losing our woods, and there was a great revival of afforestation. This spread to England, and now to-day there is a Government Forestry Department which is doing excellent work.

I remember at that time paying a visit to some of the great forests of Southern Germany, and being amazed by the skill with which they were conserved. Alas! I am afraid that is no longer so, for one hears of wholesale and indiscriminate cutting of that splendid timber as part of Germany's war preparations.

Then I went to South Africa, and there we had a different problem. There were splendid forests of native timber along the coast line, but all the tableland of the Orange River Colony and the Transvaal was bare of woods, and our task there was to plant, plant without ceasing—chiefly quick-growing things like blue gum and mimosa, in order to prevent the desiccation of the land. There I learned the dual problem which is before every country. It has to conserve wisely the forest wealth which it possesses, and in certain parts it must introduce trees where there were none before. That dual problem is before Canada to-day.

No doubt we have made many blunders—very natural blunders. Our first settlers had to clear the land for agriculture, and to them the forest was not a friend but an enemy. We have been very wasteful in that clearing. There are parts of the splendid farm lands of Ontario which have been denuded of timber. and where we have to retrace our steps and plant where our forefathers cut and slashed. But I think that we may fairly say that to-day Canada is alive to the problem. We realise that our forest wealth, to be a continuous possession for our people, must be jealously and scientifically cared for. We have to fight the menace of fire; we have to replant where replanting is necessary; we have to see that the second growth is properly thinned, so that trees may have a chance to grow to their proper stature. And in the Prairies we are doing our best by new planting to provide shelter belts for the farms, and to prevent that drying up of the soil which is a menace to our great western wheat lands.

So Canada's forest problem to-day is three-fold.

First we have to fight the dreadful peril of fire. I think this work is being done on the right lines and is improving every year. Fires are a terrible fact, but it is not always easy to determine the liability. A careless lumberman or trapper or tourist may be the cause, but it may be an act of God. I remember hearing the Chief Justice of England once say that nothing surprised him more than to find that in cases of collisions between automobiles both cars would be shown, by unanswerable evidence, to have been stationary, to have been drawn up on the right side of the road, and to have been loudly sounding their horns! That is what happens, it seems to me, in most cases when you try to enquire into the liability for a forest fire. But the menace remains, and it can only be met in two ways—by an elaborate system of fire protection with proper observation posts and proper wardens, so that a fire may be extinguished before it has gone too far; and in the second place by educating our citizens in the need for care.

I was delighted to find in northern British Columbia two years ago a vigorous organisation of young people, under the auspices of your Association, sworn to the task of fire protection. I hope, too, for great things from our National Forestry Programme, under which summer camps of young men are instructed in the elements of forestry. I visited one or two such camps last summer and was immensely struck not only by the excellence of the training, but by the wonderful effect it had upon the physique and the morale of our youth. I hope to live to see the day when the whole of our Canadian people will be forest-conscious, and every man whose dwelling is near the woods will be a skilled voluntary warden.

The second problem is wise cutting. Cutting there must be, and on a large scale, for we are entitled to reap the fruits of our forest wealth provided we do not impoverish our successors. We cannot let timber get over-ripe. I remember, on going through the Tweedsmuir Park in northern British Columbia two years ago, being shocked to see how three out of four of the enormous trees had gone rotten and were rapidly killing the fourth. But our cutting must be skilful and it must not be wasteful. It must always have behind it a purpose of conservation, and we must always be mindful of those who come after us, and realise that Canada is a concern which is not going to be wound up in a few years, but will, by God's grace, endure for many centuries.

Lastly our problem is new planting. I have seen some excellent work in this line done in Ontario, and I have seen some excellent work done in the Prairies. Farmers should be encouraged not only to handle skilfully all the timber they possess, but to do fresh planting in the interests of agriculture itself. I have seen farms in the Prairies which a decade ago were wind-swept barrens and are now surrounded by pleasant woods, with the natural accompaniment of lawns and gardens. There is no part of Canada where a farm should be merely a collection of shacks in a bare desert. Everywhere, I believe, with good advice and with reasonable care, you can by planting, not only improve the agricultural value, but enormously increase the amenities of life.

Gentlemen, I have offered you a few remarks which are not those of the expert. I am no expert, but I am profoundly convinced of the greatness of our forestry resources, of the need for their wise conservation, and of the possibility of accomplishing it. Such work should be not only an addition to our material balance sheet, but should be a real addition to our moral and spiritual assets, for it may be made a wonderful method for the training of our youth. We have to take pains with our youth. If we are to rise to our full stature as a nation we have to see that our young men are given the chance of an adequate training before they face this difficult world. We are an open-air people; our youth is an open-air youth; let us enlist its loyalty to those noble forests which are one of the principal glories of this land.

SCOTLAND

1[1]

IN MOST of the British Dominions the St. Andrew's Day banquet is the most important function of the year, for, like the Guildhall banquet in London, it is the occasion on which statesmen declare their policy. Here in Canada it has a special meaning. It is the praiseworthy custom of our race, by whatever waters of Babylon their tents may be pitched, to form a Society to remind them of their ancient home. But I doubt if the Red river and the Assiniboine can be called the waters of Babylon, for Canada, in one sense, is simply Scotland writ large. Since I came here a year ago I have never suffered for one moment from homesickness. I find pine forests and swift streams, and trout, and salmon, and mountains, which are Scotland on a grander scale; and I find in parts of the Prairies green rolling hills like my own Borders. I find everywhere men and women of Scots descent who still, after several generations, often retain the soft Highland voice or the broad Lowland speech. I have now been a good deal up and down Canada, and everywhere I go I am greeted by the sound of the pipes. You need only the heather and a Scots mist to make the resemblance complete.

Nevertheless to-night I am addressing a gathering of exiles—contented exiles—and some whose exile now dates back over many generations; but exiles all the same. For any man who has Scottish blood in his veins

[1]*St. Andrew's Day. Winnipeg. 30th November, 1936.*

is an exile away from Scotland. Now, in a sense it is the genius of the Scot to be an exile. He is extraordinarily good at pitching his tent in faraway places and prospering. But he always keeps one eye and a considerable part of his mind on the little country he has left. That is the one secret of the power of the Scot. No people, I think, since the ancient Greeks has been at once so tenacious of memories and loyalties, and at the same time so readily adaptable to new conditions.

Sometimes, in moments of despondency, I have a notion that Scotland is changing, that Scotsmen are changing, that the Scotland of to-day is very different from the country I knew when I was a boy. That, I suppose, is a malady which attacks every conservative soul as he watches the progress of time. But I comfort myself with the reflection that there are certain things in our race which can never change. We may cease to be Bible-reading and God-fearing; we may cease to be logical; we may even cease, by a fortunate dispensation, to be drouthy; but two things we will always be—far-wandering and clannish. I do not think that any process of evolution will expel from our blood the old instinct for adventure and enterprise. We shall always be like Saul looking for his father's asses with half a hope that we may find a kingdom. And I think that we shall always be clannish. We shall always cherish that warm and intimate sense of kinship which is our peculiar glory.

There are many things to be said against us—how many only a Scotsman knows. We are sometimes a little too proud of our own things merely because they are our own. And I am afraid we may also be charged sometimes with being too well satisfied, not only with

our own things, but with ourselves. My father used to
tell how, as a very young man, he wandered into a
religious meeting where, bench by bench, people were
confessing their sins. At last it came to the turn of an
old Scotsman with a shaven upper lip and a beard under
his chin. He rose and declared that he had been deeply
interested in what he had heard, and that he would only
have been too glad himself to oblige in the same way.
"But," he added, "honesty compels me to admit that
my own life for the past three years has been, humanly
speaking, pairfect." We are all apt sometimes to
claim—humanly speaking—perfection.

But, having conceded so much to the Devil's ad-
vocate, I am not prepared to concede any more. It is a
high privilege to have Scottish blood, but it is a privilege
which involves a heavy responsibility, for we have a
reputation to keep up.

Partly it is an absurd reputation. We are supposed
to be dour and hard; that may be so, but we are also
exceedingly sentimental. We are supposed to be careful
about money. No doubt we are. But in any case
which touches our heart or imagination we can be
crazily generous. We are pragmatists and realists and
critical of folly; but we are also dreamers. We are a
reverent people, and yet we can be exceedingly free
with our sacred things, as anyone who has read half a
dozen Covenanting sermons will admit. During the
debates in the presbyteries before Church union in
Scotland came about, there was one elder who finally
withdrew his opposition in these words:— "I think the
scheme of union is impracticable, ill-considered, unjust,
and indeed absolutely idiotic—but there is no doubt it
is God's will." Even in our most serious and solemn
moods we have touches of comedy. We are a law-

abiding people, because we know the value of law and order, and yet there is no race in the world which has so little real respect for constituted authorities. We accept them as an inevitable convention, but we refuse to do more than that. We are free thinkers in the best sense of the word. There was an old shoemaker in Fife who, when in a theological argument he was confronted with a quotation from the Apostle Paul, used to declare that that was just where he and Paul differed.

What the Scotsman is, only the Scotsman knows, and he will not tell. If I had to take a type of our countrymen I would take someone like Bailie Nicol Jarvie in *Rob Roy*, a respectable Glasgow merchant, very keen on business and very careful about the pennies; but ready to make a wild journey at the call of friendship, and capable, at the clachan of Aberfoyle, of seizing the red-hot coulter of a plough and turning it on the Highland cateran.

The privilege of our blood, as I have said, carries with it its duties. Sir Walter Scott once said of somebody—I think it was Lord Jeffrey—that he had "lost the broad Scots and won only the narrow English." Now there is such a thing as the narrow Scots, and that is every bit as bad as the narrow English. We are a people with a rich and varied history—a strong people made up of many diverse types—with a generous tradition behind us containing many things which dull folk consider contradictions. We have quixotry in our blood as well as prudence; poetry as well as prose. The man who tries to whittle down our heritage, to narrow our tradition, to select capriciously from our national life, is no lover of the broad Scots. We have a tradition to preserve, the full tradition. That is the first of our responsibilities.

We have also a duty to the home of those traditions—our birthplace or the birthplace of our fathers. I want to see Scotsmen all over the world maintaining a lively interest in Scotland. I do not want men of our race merely to be distinguished up and down the face of the earth; I want Scotland herself, the home of our race, to be healthy and prosperous and to retain its historic national character. There are many things amiss in Scotland to-day. We are losing some of the best of our people. We are losing especially some of the best of our rural stocks. I know glens in the Borders which, in my childhood, had half a dozen chimneys smoking, while to-day the only inhabitants are a shepherd and his dog. Some of our institutions seem to be decaying. The Scottish Bar is not what it was. The Scottish Church has not its old hold over the people. Our ancient idiomatic system of education is changing, perhaps not for the better. Too many Scottish industries are controlled from outside. Our old habits, our old tastes are changing, and, to take one instance, the Scottish vernacular is no longer spoken by us as our fathers spoke it.

Some of these changes are inevitable, but many are not. We do not want to see Scotland become merely a northern province of England. We do not want to be like the Jews of the Dispersion, a race with no Jerusalem. Therefore I would plead with those of Scottish blood to maintain a lively interest not only in their race, but in their fatherland. They can do an enormous amount by their friendly interest to preserve Scotland's individuality. Often the most idiomatic things of a country are cherished more reverently by her sons who settle abroad than by her actual inhabitants. I have found, for example, in Canada much to remind me, not of the Scotland of to-day, but of the Scotland of my boyhood. Scottish Canadians can do a very great deal to preserve the Scottish idiom in literature and in life. We want to realise that Scotland is more than a toast, that it is a real thing, a country, a home; and we must remember her not only when we are dining in her honour on St. Andrew's night, or on the birthday of Robert Burns.

There is one final duty, the most important of all. We Scots have always been exponents of unity. We learned from bitter experience in our history the evils of disunion. For hundreds of years we impoverished ourselves fighting the English, until we were fortunate enough to set a Scotsman on the English throne. But there is a greater unifying exploit in our history than even the union with England, important though that was, and that was the union of Scotsmen with each other. Do you realise that until a century or two ago the Highlands and the Lowlands were two separate peoples? Though they were nominally under the same king they had different economic interests, different social traditions, different religious creeds. And then, after 1745 and the fall of the Jacobite cause, with immense difficulty and with immense suffering these two separate races were made one nation.

To-day that union is complete. If I meet a man from Badenoch and a man from Northumberland in a foreign land, though I cannot speak the Highlander's tongue, and though the Northumbrian speaks almost with my own accent, yet I know that the first is somehow a kinsman and that the other is only a friend. The Scots tradition, the Scots character, has become one and indivisible. That is a fact which we too often forget, and it is one of the miracles of history. Two hostile peoples with utterly different traditions, and with a long record of ill-will behind them, had to wait until a century or two ago before the barriers were broken down. By a happy chance in their mingling they preserved what was best in each tradition. To-day when we sorrow for our dead it is all one whether the strain is the Lowland "Flowers of the Forest" or the Highland "Lochaber no More", the burden is the same. It is the Highland pipes that have played our Lowland soldiers into desperate battles, and in hours of recreation it is the words of an Ayrshire ploughman with which everywhere we commemorate friendship. When we praise famous men and great deeds, we do not stop to ask whether they are Lowland or Highland—it is enough for us that they are Scottish.

Having done so much, it is our duty to do more. I do not believe that the unifying power of our race is exhausted. To-day unity is the crying need of the world; unity instead of antagonism; co-operation instead of rivalry. We need a union of classes in Canada, in Britain, in the Empire. We need, if I may venture to say so, in this Dominion of ours, a closer unity where national interests are supreme above local interests. We need, above all, a unity in spirit of the nations of the world, for that is the only pathway to peace. Is it fantastic to believe that to help in the achievement of such unity is the first and greatest duty of those of Scottish blood wherever on the globe their lot may be cast? As a race we have learned the folly of division; as a race we have already achieved miracles of comprehension. In the intricate and perilous problems of to-day let us make our Scottish tradition an inspiration and an example.

2[1]

I T IS a privilege and a pleasure to join in the celebra-
tion of St. Andrew's Day in a place which, during
my sojourn in Canada, I have come to regard as my
home town. I am often invited to attend celebrations
of the jubilee or the semi-jubilee of this or that institution. Now St. Andrew's Day comes once a year, and
yet, such is the fervour of our patriotism, we always
manage to make of it a kind of jubilee, an occasion when
we look back proudly to the past and forward confidently to the future. It is written in the Book of
Leviticus that a jubilee must be ushered in with the
blowing of trumpets. Well, I do not think we ever fail
to obey that scriptural command. On St. Andrew's
Day we have a great blowing of trumpets.

To-night I am going to begin by doing something
very different. In order to propitiate the gods I propose to begin by confessing our faults. For we Scotsmen
are not infallible; we would be very unpleasant people
if we were. I remember once a speaker in the House of
Commons in England talking of what he called "that
rare and lovable character, an incompetent Scotsman".
Rare, perhaps, but lovable. If we were all that we
sometimes claim to be at our national festivals we
should certainly not be lovable. We should be violently
unpopular wherever we went, and that I do not think
we are. We know that we are far from perfect, and
I propose that we should confess our faults to-night in

[1]St. Andrew's Day. Ottawa. 30th November, 1938.

the famous words of the English mayor, "without partiality on the one hand or impartiality on the other."

Our besetting sin, I think, is that we have what is called too good a conceit of ourselves. We are inclined to accept the second- or the third-rate and praise it unduly, merely because it is our own. We have great poetry in Scotland, but we have also some very bad poetry which has been popular with Scotsmen simply because it is Scottish. It is the same thing with many other forms of art, like music and painting. It is true also of much of our philosophy, and much of our theology, and we are inclined, I think, to judge small defects more lightly in our countrymen than in other people. Now the reason for this critical laxity is not that we lack critical power and sound standards, but that we are sentimentally clannish and have a sincere affection for our own folk. We were always a little country, and for long we were a very poor country, and to keep going we had to hold together. The Scottish family was a remarkably close corporation. There is a story of a man who had lived for a long time with his sister; he married a wife, and the sister went on living in the same house. Someone observed that this was a rather awkward situation for the new wife. "D'you think," said the husband, "that I would put away my ain sister for the sake of a strange woman?" The compactness of the family extended to the village, the burgh, the clan, and ultimately to the nation. We are desperately interested in our own people. Sydney Smith, you remember, once said that he wished he had been born a Scotsman, for then so many other Scotsmen would have taken an interest in him.

No doubt this is a fault, but I am inclined to think

it is rather a venial fault, and moreover it is a fault which leads to much good comedy. We Scotsmen are always apt to claim anybody who does anything remarkable as a member of our race, often on slender grounds. About thirty years ago an eminent figure appeared in China called Yuan-Shih Kai. I believe that the folk in Sutherland were convinced that this was one Euan McKay who had gone East from those parts some twenty years before. During the French Revolution the name of Robespierre became famous over all the world. The citizens of Glasgow believed that this was a certain Rob Speir, a defaulting lawyer who had disappeared some years before from the city. The classic case is that of the Scotsman who claimed most of the great men of history as Caledonians until he was confronted with Shakespeare. "There," said his cross-examiner, "at any rate you cannot claim that Shakespeare was a Scot." The answer was, "I admit there is no direct evidence, but surely his great ability warrants the assumption?" Best of all I like the story of the provost of my little Border burgh a hundred years ago, who attended the great dinner given in London to celebrate the passing of the First Reform Bill. He looked upon the wine when it was red and became rather confused, so when the main toast— "The Majesty of the People"—was proposed, I think by Lord Brougham, he rose to reply, under the impression that the toast was "the Magistrates of Peebles". It seemed to his honest mind that that was a toast which might well be drunk in the metropolis by this great assembly of the leading men of Britain!

Well, I have done with our confession of sins, and I proceed to a modest blowing of trumpets. The curious thing is that our chief virtue, I think, as a nation is just

the opposite of our besetting sin. If we are too clannish, too apt to combine in a too rigid social unit, we
are also extraordinarily good at standing alone. Our
patron saint is St. Andrew; it might well be St. Athana-
sius, who, you remember, was famous for being "contra
mundum". If we depend a good deal upon our kin we
are exceedingly independent of the rest of the world.
There is a famous sentence of Sir Walter Scott's: "I
was born a Scotsman and a bare one. Therefore I was
born to fight my way in the world—with my left hand
if my right hand fail me, and with my teeth if both were
cut off." Perhaps it was the vicissitudes of our history;
perhaps it was the rigours of our northern climate;
perhaps it was the pressure of poverty; but we have
never been afraid to take risks, or, as our proverb has
it, "to put a stout heart to a stey brae." Our motto
might be that of my Border town, which carries in its
coat-of-arms three salmon, two of them with their
heads turned upstream, and the motto: *Contra nando
incrementum*—"by swimming against the current we
increase."

I think this national characteristic of ours is of extraordinary value in the world we live in to-day. I
remember once in Scotland going with my hostess to
call at a neighbouring house. The old butler who came
to the door, shook his head and said that he was afraid
the laird could see nobody, for he was far from well.
When my hostess enquired sympathetically what the
ailment was, the old man replied, "Weel, my leddy, you
see the colonel is a perfect martyr to deleerium tremens". I think we might say that the world to-day is
a martyr to delirium tremens—a martyr, for it is not
altogether the poor world's blame that it suffers from
that painful complaint. One of the symptoms is that

people are afraid to stand on their own feet. They seem to want to huddle together for security, and to sell their souls to a dictator or to a machine. I cannot quite see our Scottish countrymen following this example. He would be a very unhappy dictator who tried the game with us.

But there is another thing as dangerous as this craving for a base security by surrendering freedom, and that is the modern craze for false doctrines—what the jargon of to-day calls "ideologies", creeds which seem to be accepted with a passionate devotion, as if they were new revelations, but which for the most part are the oldest of heresies, which were centuries ago exploded and discarded. I think that as a race we are too critical, and we have too much common-sense to fall under the bondage of those ancient follies which have been resurrected from their dishonoured graves. Our attitude to them will, I hope, always be that which was well expressed by a Highland game-keeper in conversation with a friend of mine who was shooting capercailzie on Spey-side. The capercailzie, as you know, is a large bird which is found in the Highland forests; it is not very easy to kill and not very good to eat. My friend asked the keeper, "What do you do with a capercailzie when you have shot it?" "Weel," was the answer, "ye roll it up in brown paper and bury it for a week." "And then?" my friend asked. "Ye dig it up." "And then?" "And then," said the man, "if ye've ony sense ye bury it again."

3[1]

I WONDER if any of you have attended the function known as the Manufacturers' Dinner in Galashiels? The meal begins at five or six o'clock and goes on until after midnight, and there are usually about forty toasts! On one occasion an old farmer from far up in the glens of Ettrick arose about half past eleven. He said, "The toast with which I have been entrusted is the Clergy of a' Denominations. . . . My freends, we ken them fine. They're a wheen dismal bodies." To-night I feel inclined to adapt that classic formula to the toast which I have to propose. My toast is the Scottish Curlers. We ken them fine. They're a wheen decent bodies."

I need not tell you how glad I am to see you here. Curling and golf are Scotland's two chief contributions to the relaxation of humanity. By the way it is odd how little either of them has entered into Scottish literature. Burns could have written a great curling poem, but he never tried, except in the opening stanzas of "Tam Samson's Elegy". You remember how they go—

> "When Winter muffles up his cloak,
> And binds the mire up like a rock;
> When to the lochs the curlers flock,
>   Wi' gleesome speed,
> Wha will they station at the cock?—
>   Tam Samson's dead!

[1]*Dinner to the Scottish Curlers. Ottawa. January, 1938.*

He was the king o' a' the core,
To guard, or draw, or wick a bore;
Or up the rink like Jehu roar
        In time o' need;
But now he lags on Death's hog-score—
        Tam Samson's dead!''

When I was a boy in Tweeddale, and hard winters
were more common in Scotland than they are to-day, I
remember many happy hours when the whole countryside gathered to the local mill dam. It was a wonderful
example of true democracy, for there you had the
minister, in moments of excitement, weeping on the
shoulder of the local ne'er-do-weel, and the sheriff
wringing the hand of the local poacher whom in a week
or two he was to sentence to sixty days. Curling
obliterated all restrictions of class, education and character in a common sporting interest. I do not suppose
I shall ever again have such an appetite for a meal as
I had for what we called "curlers' fare"—boiled beef
and greens. To-day things are very different. Artificial
ice is the rule, and the curlers do not congregate at the
mill dam, but go in by the morning train to Edinburgh.
No doubt in art and skill much has been gained, but
something, too, has been lost.

Scotland may be the birthplace of curling, but I
fancy Canada to-day is its chief home. You will see
many strange and novel things in Canada. For one
thing you will see the proper kind of winter, where
there is nothing half-hearted about the frost and snow.
You will see other novelties. When my fellow Borderer,
Lord Minto, was Governor-General here, he had the
pleasure of entertaining a Scottish curling team. In
our dry electric air it is possible to light the gas by
placing a finger on the jet, and there used to be a jet
kept in Rideau Hall for the purpose. This was pointed

out to one of the visitors, who duly performed the feat.
He observed that "it cowed a'." "When I get hame,"
he said, "I'll hae some queer things to tell the wife, but
I'll no tell her that. She would say I had been drinkin'."
You will see another novelty. In the Ottawa and St.
Lawrence valleys we curl not with the familiar "channel-
stanes", but with mighty discs of iron, which personally I find hard to manage. I am told that this
practice originated with the British regiments who in
the old days garrisoned certain Canadian cities. Being
far from Crawfordjohn they could not get the proper
"channel-stanes", so they seem to have followed the
Scriptural injunction—not beating their swords into
ploughshares, but beating their antiquated guns into
the implements of curling!

I need not tell you how much I hope that you will
enjoy your time here and keep up the honour of
Scotland. I do not mean that I want you to beat the
Canadian rinks, for Canada for the moment is my
adopted country; but I want you to give a good account
of yourselves, as I am sure you will.

You will carry back many messages to our native
land. You will tell them that you have met Scotsmen
everywhere in Canada. Many parts of the Dominion
are more Scottish, I think, than Scotland. Down in
Cape Breton you will hear nearly as much Gaelic as in
Sutherland or the Isles. And you will tell them at
home that our countrymen are not only loyal and
vigorous Canadian citizens, but that they do not forget
the rock whence they were hewn. You will find that
Scotsmen settled here, settled even for many generations, still cherish a warm affection for their land of
origin.

III

OUR NEIGHBOURS

Mr. Roosevelt at Quebec[1]

MR. PRESIDENT, as the personal representative of His Majesty the King I offer my most cordial greetings to the First Citizen of the United States. Canada welcomes you, sir, not only for your own sake as an old acquaintance—for I think you know well our Eastern coasts—but also as one of the major forces to-day in the statesmanship of the world. She welcomes you not less as the head of a country to whose people she is bound by ties of kinship and tradition; a country whose problems she shares, and whose future deeply concerns her own. As a North American nation, we have much in common with you; yet we have each our own idioms and characteristics. Our differences, understood and respected, are, not less than our similarities, a basis for co-operation and friendship.

Canada is a free and a sovereign nation and for generations she has dwelt side by side with yours in perfect amity—an example to all the world. She is also a principal constituent part of the British Empire, and as such she is a link between your great Republic and that Commonwealth of Nations which covers so large a part of the habitable globe. Mr. President, it is my earnest hope—and I know that it is also yours—that our friendship and good-will may grow into a still closer understanding, and become that strongest of human creations, a thing about which men do not argue but which they can take for granted. It is my prayer that,

[1] *31st July, 1936.*

57

not by any alliance, political or otherwise, but through thinking the same thoughts and pursuing the same purpose, the Republic of the United States and the British Commonwealth may help to restore the shaken liberties of mankind.

THE GOVERNOR-GENERAL AT WASHINGTON

On Thursday, April 1st, 1937, the Senate of the United States adjourned in order to welcome the Governor-General of Canada. The Vice-President then asked the Governor-General to address the House.

MR. VICE-PRESIDENT and Senators, you have done me to-day a great kindness and a great honour, for which I am deeply grateful. This is the culminating stage in what has been a most memorable visit. I have had the opportunity, in a city which I used to know well, of renewing many old friendships and making some new ones.

I am told, Senators, that I am supposed to say something to you to-day. A Governor-General is in a very curious position. Once I was like you: I was a free and independent politician. I could liberate my mind on any subject, anywhere, at any time, at any length I pleased. I had an official character and, like you, I had also a private character. I need not remind you that a man's official character does not as a rule do justice to the stalwart virtues which he possesses as a private citizen. I remember in my own country of the Scottish Borders there was an old minister who once a month thought it his duty to deliver a sermon upon the terrors of Hell, when he fairly dangled his congregation over the abyss. But, being a humane man, he liked to finish on a gentler note. He used to conclude thus: "Of course, my friends, ye understand that the Almighty is

59

compelled to do things in his official capacity that he would scorn to do as a private individual."

Now, I am in the unfortunate position of having no private capacity, but only an official one. I am unable to express my views upon any public question of real importance—at least, not for publication. But there is one subject on which even a Governor-General may speak freely, and that is my gratitude for your kindness here and my admiration for your great country. I have known the United States for many years. I have had the privilege of the friendship of many of your citizens. I have long been a student of your history. I am very sure that no American steeped in European history gets a greater thrill from Westminster Abbey than I get from Valley Forge and the Wilderness of Virginia, and the Shenandoah.

I have always believed that the future of civilisation lies principally in the hands of the English-speaking peoples. I want these great nations not only to speak the same language, but to think along the same lines. For that is the only true form of co-operation. If I may venture to say so, far too much is said about my country and your country being alike. It is much more important that they should be different. The strength of an alliance between two nations lies in the fact that they should be complementary to each other and each give to the other something new. Therefore, I am inclined to rejoice when I find a real difference in your country and mine.

But I think, when that has been said, that we have a wonderful basis for thinking together and working together. In the first place we have the same definition of what constitutes greatness and goodness in human character. We admire the same qualities. We give our

admiration and affection to the same type of leadership. Will anyone deny that your great men and our
great men are singularly alike? In the second place we
and you have the same task before us.   In Canada
nearly all our problems are paralleled by your own.
We have the same economic problems. We have the
same problems in the drought areas of the West. We
have very similar constitutional problems, and we have
the task of harmonising local interests and rights with
national interests and duties.

Senators, I cannot imagine a greater bond between
two nations than that they should be engaged in the
same tasks and for the same purpose.

CANADA AND THE UNITED STATES[1]

IT IS a happy chance for me that has brought this Conference to a city on Canadian soil. As you know, a Governor-General is not wholly free in his movements. He cannot slip across the border when he pleases, for he is hedged around with official formalities. Now, the United States has long been to me a second homeland. When I came to Canada I hoped to see much of them and their people. Well, if Mahomet cannot go to the mountain, the mountain, on this occasion, has been obliging enough to come to Mahomet. I rejoice in this opportunity of meeting some of my American friends.

I cannot praise too highly the enterprise of which this Conference is the fruit. We are good neighbours—we have been good neighbours for more than a century and, please God, we shall always set an example to the world of how civilised peoples can live together. But just as in private life friendship is a thing which must be cultivated if it is to endure, so between nations there must be a continuous effort towards a better comprehension. It was Dr. Johnson who said that a man should keep his friendships in constant repair. New problems, new modes of thought, are always arising, and it is vital that each should keep in touch with the development of the other.

In these conferences you discuss historical influences which have not lost their power; you discuss problems in politics, in economics, in education, which Canada

[1]*Canadian-American Conference. Kingston, Ont. 17th June, 1937.*

shares with the United States. On many of these it would not be fitting for me to express an opinion. Man, according to Aristotle, is a political animal, but there is an exception in the case of a Governor-General. His views on public policy can only be the views of his Ministers. If he touches on the subject he must confine himself to what may be called Governor-Generalities. He represents the King; the King, by an axiom of our constitutional law, can do no wrong; therefore neither King nor Governor-General can be a politician. But I can assure you that I have read the record of your Conference last year with profound interest and advantage, and I am looking forward this year to the same pleasure.

To-day I will say nothing of the substance of your discussions, but I should like to submit to you a point of view. I believe—I have always believed—that on a close understanding between the British Commonwealth and the Republic of the United States depends the peace and freedom of the world. I say understanding, not alliance. What matters is that we should think on the same lines, not that we should tie ourselves up in any formal treaty. The instinct to avoid formal commitments, to feel our way cautiously and let facts shape our course, is deep in our common heritage. It is a sound instinct. It is exemplified in the American dislike of what they call "entangling alliances," and in that astonishingly elastic instrument, our British constitution. It is a common spirit, similar modes of thought, the same purpose and ideals, that make the true basis for co-operation. Let me give you two recent examples. The League of Nations was based upon a legal treaty in the shape of the Covenant, a scheme of obligations buttressed by weighty sanctions.

But in the crisis of eighteen months ago it was discovered that the Covenant would not work, simply because there was not any true identity of purpose in the nations which composed the League. Take an instance on the other side. Under the Statute of Westminster the British Dominions are free and sovereign nations, linked together only by a common tradition and a common Crown. Yet in the difficult situation which arose at the close of last year the members of the Commonwealth spoke with one voice. Why? Because they thought on the same lines, and had behind them what is far more vital than any constitutional bond, a serious unity of spirit.

I believe that the omens are good for this mutual comprehension between the American Republic and our Commonwealth. You must have been struck, gentlemen, as I have been, by the close inter-connection in those relations for which I must use the ugly word "cultural." A new fashion, say, in American fiction, finds at once its imitators in Britain; a new development in our novel has immediate followers in the United States. The modern American school of poetry is influencing ours and being influenced in turn. It is the same with philosophy and the different branches of science; any fresh movement in either country has at once its repercussions in the other. There is no other pair of nations so closely linked together. Take France, which is only fifty miles or so from the British coast, while America is over two thousand. French literature and thought have of course their influence on us, and ours on France, but there is always a considerable time-lag. But with Britain and America the reactions are profound and immediate. With such a basis of receptivity, my hope is that more and more we shall pool our ideas on all matters concerning our peace, until out of the exchange shall come a fuller understanding and a common creed.

I have spoken of Britain, since Britain is still the centre of the Commonwealth of which Canada is a distinguished part. Now let me speak of the land in which I have the honour to represent the King. Canada is a North American nation with a jealously maintained European connection. She has therefore many problems in common with the United States, and certain others due to her membership of the British Empire. That is to say, she has affiliations with the world at large which differentiate her from other North American peoples. She can never be quite like her neighbour, and that is all to the good, for it means that she has a specific contribution of her own to make to North American civilisation.

I like to think of her, with her English and French peoples, as in a special degree the guardian of the great Mediterranean tradition which descends from Greece and Rome, and which she has to mould to the uses of a new world. I want to see her keep her clear-cut individuality, for that is of inestimable advantage, not only to her, but to her neighbour. There is far more hope of effective co-operation between nations which are not too much alike, but which understand and respect each other's stalwart idiosyncrasies. We in Canada get a great deal from the United States, most of it good, some of it, like all borrowings, not so good. I believe that the time will come when the United States will get a good deal from us. Sometimes I hear pessimists here complain of the dangerous influence of the United States on Canada. Some day I hope pessimists on the other side of the border-line will talk

of the dangerous influence of Canada on the United
States. And then I shall die happy.

For Canada has much to give. Some of her assets
are already understood. She is becoming a favourite
holiday-land for her neighbours. She can still offer a
physical frontier, a border-line beyond which little is
known, and it is many a day since the United States
lost that supreme attraction for the young and the
adventurous. She has a mysterious North Land which
I believe will become the home of new industries and
new modes of life. She has, in her French inhabitants,
an enclave of an elder Europe; you do not need to cross
the Atlantic to learn the spell of the Old World. We
send our young men to the great schools and colleges
of the United States. I want to see that compliment
returned, for though we have less than one-twelfth of
the numbers of our neighbours, we have no mean
educational apparatus. We have medical schools which
can hold their own with any on the globe; in me allurgy
and mineralogy we are fast developing a notable technique; our transport problems are as intricate and as
interesting as ever faced a nation; and for the student
of law we have the Civil Law not only studied here but
practised. The business relations between Canada and
the United States are close and fast growing; I want to
see a similar development in the commerce of ideas and
knowledge.

One last word. We in Canada have one most potent
bond with our southern neighbour. We are engaged in
the same job. Both, in a sense, are young nations
which have not yet reached complete maturity and
integration. Henry James, in that wonderful and subtle
study of his native land which he wrote after his last
visit in 1905, has a passage in which he says that he

often wished that his country could have the "close and complete consciousness of the Scots". (I pause to observe that I cannot imagine a more nightmare conception than that America should have the close, compact nationalism of the Scots. What would happen to the world if you had 120 million Scotsmen living in the same country?) We in Canada are in much the same position. We have both of us great territories which we have no desire to add to in bulk. Our task is to develop them for the purposes of a civilised life. It is a great task, and a difficult task, but can there be any closer link between two peoples than that they should be engaged in the same work? We have learned in recent years, both of us, I think, the transience of mere material wealth and the transcendent importance of the spirit of man. The duty of both nations is to vindicate that spirit against the dead weight of circumstance, to integrate ourselves and our possessions, and to establish that balance of law and liberty which is the only meaning of democracy and of civilisation.

IV

THE SERVICE OF THE STATE

The Service of the State[1]

I HAVE the privilege tonight of addressing an audience largely young, whose hopes in life are not yet dimmed by disappointments, and to whom as to Ancient Pistol the world is an oyster waiting to be opened. So I am going to offer to you a plea that one consideration should be present when you plan your careers. It is that you should remember that you are not only individuals but also citizens. It is that in all your schemes some allowance should be made for that supreme duty, a duty second only to that which a man owes to his soul, and which I shall call the service of the State. It is obvious that no nation can be strong unless it can enlist for national purposes the help of its best citizens. You educated young men and women are the cream of that citizenship. It is only if you are willing to give, each in different degrees, thought and work to the welfare of the nation that your country will achieve that greatness which every patriot desires.

Let me begin by paying a tribute to a certain British tradition. Heaven knows that some of our British traditions are foolish enough! but there is one which has now persisted for more than two centuries, and which has been of incalculable value to us in recent difficult days. That tradition is that the public service is one of the most honourable of all pursuits. It takes many forms. When I was an undergraduate at Oxford some of the ablest men in each year went naturally into the Civil Service; not because of the pecuniary rewards,

[1]*University of Manitoba. Winnipeg. December, 1936.*

though these were reasonably adequate at the start; but because of its dignity and interest. I say dignity and interest, for it was this, I think, rather than any stern sense of duty, which determined their choice. I am glad to think that this excellent habit still continues. Our home Civil Service is recruited from the ablest men in the Universities. Our Indian and Colonial Services are recruited from the most enterprising. The service of the State has, in the eyes of the ordinary Englishman, a distinction of its own which outweighs the solemn fact that no one will make a fortune in it.

That is one side of the tradition. On the other side, service in Parliament has a notable prestige. A successful business man looks to a seat in the House as the crown of his career. An able young man, going to the Bar, in nine cases out of ten looks forward ultimately to entering Parliament. When I was in the House of Commons there were at least a score of eldest sons of famous families who had come naturally into the House, and who worked very hard at their parliamentary duties. That, you will say, is due to the fact that we have a large leisured class whose eldest sons are not compelled to struggle for their daily bread. Yes, but there is more in it than that. Why should a rich young man, with every opportunity for amusement elsewhere, be so ready to devote himself to a calling which has more kicks than ha'pence in it, which is always laborious and often unpleasant? Look at our list of Under-Secretaries in Britain to-day and you will find among them a very large number of young men who, in other countries, would never dream of undertaking the toil and disappointments of parliamentary life.

No doubt there are baser elements in the tradition. There is personal ambition, for example, which may be much stronger than any sense of public duty. There is a certain tincture of snobbishness, a desire to be a member of the governing classes. But when all that has been admitted there is something fine and worthy about the instinct, for there is no pecuniary motive in it. The financial rewards held out by the public service in Britain are trivial indeed compared with those of commercial and professional careers. Deep down there is a sound instinct that there is something honourable in serving the State. I do not think it possible to exaggerate the value of this tradition in the Mother Country. It has given us a most competent, single-hearted and clean Civil Service. It has given us a political life in which we can honestly say that the best brains and character in the nation are represented. It has kept the prestige of our Parliament high at a time when constitutionalism elsewhere in the world has tended to fall into disrepute.

I sometimes ask myself what Britain has to offer to-day to the Dominions in the way of intellectual and moral inspiration. She has given them much in the past—a tradition of free and orderly government, and a great literature of thought and imagination. But these gifts she has made to all the world, and they are no longer looked upon as her specific bequest, since they have become part of the common stock of civilisation. When I was a young man she gave them the conception of the Empire as an organic unity, and those of my own age will remember how strong and fresh was the first impulse of that ideal. Since those days what was a novelty has become a commonplace. The doctrine remains, but it has passed into the light of common day. It is now a business policy, no longer an inspiration. The first fine rapture of it has gone, and it cannot appeal to the youth of to-day as it appealed to those of my generation, to whom it seemed a new and wonderful thing.

But some spiritual force must emanate from the Mother Country, some inspiration, some creed, or our Commonwealth will become a dull and pedestrian thing. Had it been possible for Britain to take the lead in inaugurating a new system of world peace, then we should have had something to capture the imagination and to kindle the spirit of youth. Unhappily that possibility is still remote, though we are patiently labouring towards it. Meanwhile I think that Britain can offer to the Commonwealth, and to all the world, one example which has a true spiritual value— the example of a closely integrated people among whom unselfish public service is still regarded as a supreme duty and privilege.

All democracies have not had the good fortune of Britain. In some there has been a tendency for the ablest men, the men of the highest ideals, to withdraw their skirts from practical politics as if they were an unclean thing. That meant inevitably that the whole business of government lost prestige and fell into the hands of the second and third rate. The result was not only an inadequate Civil Service, but a decline in the quality of the parliaments themselves. Moreover, there were other careers which seemed to offer greater material rewards and which attracted the abler young men. So with this combination, discredited politics and glorified business, it was impossible to enlist the best talent in the country's service. A tradition was created definitely hostile to the service of the State.

What was the consequence? No evil results were felt in the piping times of peace and prosperity. But it was different when the day of crisis came, when "rugged individualism" was no longer possible, when the horizon of enterprise narrowed, and when the immense importance of the State revealed itself with blinding clearness to those who had forgotten all about it. Men turned their eyes to the Government, and they found, as they were bound to find, the Government machine unready and inadequate, since it had long lacked the support of the best talent in the country. A new tradition had to be improvised, and it is not easy to improvise a tradition.

The moral is that if we neglect the State for our private interests there will most certainly come a day when this neglect will react most seriously upon these private interests themselves. This is not abstract idealism, but a matter of plain business. The well-being of the nation, the honest and efficient functioning of the governmental machine, is of vital import to every business man, to every professional man, to every citizen. It is of more importance to-day than ever, because, with our multitude of intricate problems and the inevitable extension of the sphere of State duties, a country's government has become an intimate concern to everybody. We cannot hold ourselves aloof from the State as our grandfathers could. Our choice is not between public and private life, for in a sense there is no more private life. An immense amount of government you must have; the alternatives are government which is confused and corrupt and government which is clean and competent.

I offer these reflections to you younger people, for I think they touch you closely. Those of you who may follow ordinary business and professional careers I would beg to remember how vitally public affairs concern you, and urge you to give them a close and vigilant attention. That is the meaning of democracy— that the whole nation concerns itself with national questions and that thereby an informed public opinion is created which is the true sovereign. To others who may not yet have chosen their calling I would like to say one word on behalf of the direct service of the State. It will not bring you great pecuniary rewards— but in these days of shifting economies it is hard to say what will bring you assured pecuniary rewards! But it will give you a life of intense interest, and a proud and honourable calling. And by the direct service of the State I do not mean only the Civil Service of Canada. I include a British Colonial Service and an Indian Service. I want to see more young Canadians in the Civil Service of the whole Empire, for that service is as much the right of Canada as it is of Britain.

And lastly to those who have the instinct and the talent I would urge the importance of a political career. Parliaments to-day have fallen in repute in many parts of the world, but in our British democracies I do not think that their prestige has been lessened—indeed I think it has increased, because we realise that what we have created we have now vigorously to defend. Democracy is a fighting creed as never before. Therefore I confess I am utterly impatient with cheap gibes at Parliament and parliamentarians. It is our British fashion not to be too respectful to our authorities, and that is all to the good, for nothing is worse for Members

of Parliament than that they should be coddled and un-
criticised. But a vigilant criticism is quite consistent
with a sincere respect. Members of Parliament to-day
are doing a great and responsible work under many
difficulties. They are the St. Sebastians of our time
stuck up in a high place to be shot full of arrows. I
want to see their prestige exalted so that brilliant
young men will regard service of that kind as in the
fullest degree worthy of them. For if Parliaments are
to continue they must represent the best that is in
every nation.

I am addressing an academic audience and I am
going to conclude by reminding you of a famous passage
in the *Republic of Plato*. In Book VII Socrates dis-
cusses the relation between the life of contemplation
and that practical business of politics which he calls
the "cave". Philosophers, he said, must return to the
task of governing. They must realise that it is a duty
which they owe to their city for the opportunity which
it has given to them to become philosophers. No doubt
it will be hard to leave the clear air of ideas for the
darkness of the cave; but they must if they are right-
thinking men. They will take office, says Glaucon, "as
a stern necessity and not like our present politicians."

It is an interesting passage for it marks the first
emergence in Plato of the idea of duty, where a man is
required to do something irrespective of his own personal good. Here the philosopher is enjoined to surrender a better life for a worse one. It is a foreshadow-
ing of the Christian doctrine that all men are members
one of another. But the most interesting point about
the passage is this. In reply to Glaucon Socrates says
that the rulers must be philosophers returning con-
sciously to the cave, that is to say, they must be men

who have already known a better life than the political—*bion ameinō tou politikou.* In a word, they must
not be mere politicians, following the game for the
game's sake and living by narrow and earthy standards.

Plato's argument still holds good. That is why it is
essential to have in the service of the State men of
culture and ideals who bring into what must always
be a dusty business the clean air and the high spirit
of a wider life. That is why we need the best of you in
politics. The greatest figures in public life have always
been those who did not pursue it for any of the obvious
shallow rewards in power or notoriety, but from a
strong sense of duty to their fellows. They may become
adepts at the game, but they must always be able to
look around it and to live outside it. The wife of a
famous Viceroy of India once said most truly that no
woman should ever be Vicereine to whom it was a
treat. I should paraphrase this and say that the best
politicians are those who would prefer to be otherwise
engaged. For that means that they will have rich and
enduring interests outside politics which will enable
them to bring fruitful minds to bear upon their problems, and, moreover, they will have no temptation to
run for common and vulgar stakes. We need in the
service of the State the best talent and the best character in the nation, and that will be found especially
among those who have already other worlds of their
own in which they are happy, and who enter this particular world primarily from a sense of duty. The
service of the State should have the highest possible
prestige, but it is not for the sake of that prestige that
it will attract the best servants.

Canada's Outlook on the World[1]

THIS is the first occasion on which I have had the privilege of meeting the members of your Institute of International Affairs. A Governor-General, I need hardly remind you, has to walk warily. In the domestic affairs of the country where he represents the King, he can have no views on policy except those of his ministers. And even on international questions he is in a position of some delicacy, for to-day international problems have the unhappy knack of also becoming domestic problems and dividing people into party groups.

So, to-night you will not hear from me any views on international policy. But there is one thing on which I can speak frankly. The purpose of your organisation is study. You are a forum for discussion, not an agency for propaganda. Your business is to acquire expert knowledge about the data on which policies must be framed. Now, that is a purpose whose value is altogether beyond question. No policy is of any use unless it is adequate to the facts, and the first duty of the citizen is to inform himself of the facts.

In the old days in Britain foreign affairs were very largely a matter of platitudes and sentiment. We were moderately disturbed by matters like the Risorgimento in Italy and by Turkish misrule in the Near East. A great orator like Mr. Gladstone could arouse the emotions of his countrymen to a high pitch over such

[1]*Anniversary Dinner of the Canadian Institute of International Affairs. Montreal. 12th October, 1937.*

matters. Foreign questions, too, now and then seemed
to threaten the safety of the Empire's frontiers, and to
arouse patriotic anxieties. But these occasions were
not very numerous. On the whole, one may say that
till thirty or forty years ago foreign affairs had only an
academic interest for the ordinary British citizen.

How different it is to-day! The world has been
telescoped, distances have shrunk, and every nation is
in some kind of uneasy bondage to the others. What is
happening three thousand miles away may have a
direct effect upon the safety and prosperity of the
private citizen. Therefore every nation must have a
foreign policy in the sense that it must consider its
position *vis-à-vis* the world at large. No country can
seclude itself and declare that it will go its own way
without troubling its head over what other people are
doing. Its political security, its economic prosperity,
compels it to have some reasoned attitude towards
the outer world.

This attitude must be mainly determined by the
citizens themselves. The day has gone when foreign
policy can be the preserve of a group of officials at the
Foreign Office, or a small social class, or a narrow
clique of statesmen from whom the rest of the nation
obediently takes its cue. To-day the problems affect
us all too vitally in our private interests. The foreign
policy of a democracy must be the cumulative views of
individual citizens, and if these views are to be sound
they must in turn be the consequence of a widely
diffused knowledge.

From this duty no country is exempt. Certainly not
Canada. She is a sovereign nation and cannot take her
attitude to the world docilely from Britain, or from the
United States, or from anybody else. A Canadian's first

loyalty is not to the British Commonwealth of Nations, but to Canada and to Canada's King, and those who deny this are doing, to my mind, a great disservice to the Commonwealth. If the Commonwealth, in a crisis, is to speak with one voice it will be only because the component parts have thought out for themselves their own special problems, and made their contribution to the discussion, so that a true common factor of policy can be reached. A sovereign people must, as part of its sovereign duty, take up its own attitude to world problems. The only question is whether that attitude shall be a wise and well-informed one or a short-sighted and ill-informed one.   Therefore we need knowledge— exact knowledge—and it is one of the objects of this Institute to provide that.

But we need something more. We must understand not only the facts about foreign nations, but their point of view. In the past we have been far too fond of blind antagonisms. The popular mind has been "pro" one nation or "anti" another, "phil" one thing or "phobe" something else, very largely out of a vague sentiment or prejudice.

That attitude is impossible to-day. Things are too serious for mere prejudice and sentiment. There is a crying need everywhere for the right kind of propaganda. Propaganda can be a horrible thing when it means the dissemination of falsehood and bitterness. But it can be a very fine thing when it is directed towards a truer understanding by the nations of each other. We in Britain have been always rather bad at the job and have despised it, and consequently a good many absurd fallacies about ourselves have grown up in foreign countries.

Now the supreme truth we have learned in recent

years has been the interconnection of nations, the community of interests of the world at large, the truth that no country is prosperous because of its neighbours' misfortunes, but only because of its neighbours' well-being. But this truth by itself is valueless unless it leads to a fuller knowledge of those neighbours who matter so much to us. We want to understand their point of view. That does not mean necessarily that we should share it, for their point of view may be wrong; but if we have to fight it, we shall fight it all the better for understanding it.

We must have more than knowledge; we must have sympathy. As someone has said, our problem is to make certain that the democracy in which we believe can live peaceably side by side with creeds which are not democratic. It is not for us to declare that we are the people, and that wisdom will die with us. Tolerance of other forms of government abroad should be part of every democrat's creed. There is a famous French proverb, "Tout comprendre c'est tout pardonner". That always seems to me slightly patronizing, and I prefer the version of Madame de Staël—"Tout comprendre nous rend très indulgents". A great German philosopher once said truly that the essence of tragedy was not a clash between right and wrong, but a clash between two rights.

I remember that my old friend, James Bryce, was never tired of insisting that there must be some element of truth, some kernel of honest idealism, in any creed which moved the heart of a large body of men, and that it was our duty to discover that kernel of truth, that element of value. That wise attitude seems to me especially important to-day. We see much in certain other countries which we dislike. But surely the right way is not blind condemnation, as if they had sold their souls to the devil. It is our business in studying the mind of foreign peoples to look for the kernel of truth, the element of value which must be there. It may be preposterously overstated, it may even be hopelessly perverted; but we shall be far better able to check its perversions and reduce folly to sanity if we recognize what is sound and true in it.

The purpose which your Institute sets before itself is not merely to provide a limited number of cultivated men and women with accurate knowledge. It will help, I trust, here and in Britain to create that spirit without which a true internationalism is impossible. The League of Nations has not succeeded as we had hoped, because it had not an adequate spiritual force behind it. No international mechanism which the wit of man can frame will succeed unless there is behind it, in the world at large, the proper temper of mind. To create and maintain this temper is the first duty of every civilised man.

LORD DURHAM[1]

I AM always happy to be present at a dinner of members of my old profession, a profession with which, as an honorary Bencher of Osgoode Hall, I am proud to have a Canadian connection. A gathering of lawyers is usually a little suspect. Do you remember an ominous sentence of Adam Smith's?—"People of the same trade seldom meet together, even for merriment and diversion, but the conversation ends in a conspiracy against the public." But to-night the public need have no fears. This is not an ordinary annual dinner of the club, for its purpose is to commemorate what happened a hundred years ago, an event which is one of the most memorable in the story of the British Empire. The year 1838 saw the issue of Lord Durham's report.

The toast with which I am entrusted to-night is in memory of Lord Durham. He died within two years of his return to England, disappointed, misunderstood, bitterly criticized, his brief career having closed in apparent failure. But his dying words were, "Canada will some day do justice to my memory," and the family motto of the Lambtons was, "Le jour viendra." That day has come. The world has long ago done ample justice to his work and he stands high on the roll of the makers of the Canadian nation.

A century is a long time, but till the other day there were men alive who had seen him. Lord Strathcona, whom I knew in my youth, once saw Durham, and was

[1]*University of Toronto Law Club Dinner. Toronto. 1938.*

reprimanded for omitting to remove his hat. What manner of man was this English peer, whose dark, eager, melancholy face looks down on us in our dining-room at Rideau Hall from the canvas of Sir Thomas Lawrence. He was that not uncommon type, the radical aristocrat. The nobleman with popular sympathies is apt to cut a slightly ridiculous figure, like the Jacobinical *ci-devants* of the French Revolution. The world, remembering the Rockinghams and Lafayettes of history, suspects a lack of humour and of common humanity. I remember Lord Rosebery once telling me that, in his early days, when he was Mr. Gladstone's chief lieutenant and the apostle of Scottish Liberalism, he was always in terror of being tarred with that brush. The reason is plain; such a type is apt to be condescending, and democracy has no use for condescension. Durham's political creed was mainly a family bequest and not altogether suited to his temperament. He was called "Radical Jack" and "The King of the Colliers," but I wonder how much he really understood that fine stock, the Durham miners! He was their master, and their patron; I doubt if he could ever have been their comrade and friend. But he had one truly liberal quality: he hated cruelty and tyranny of any kind; and he was as vehement a critic of the brutality and intimidation of the miners' unions as of the misdeeds of Tory landlords.

What was the nature of the man? There is not much to attract us in the malicious picture drawn by Charles Greville. Durham came in for a good deal of criticism in his day. He was accused of class pride and personal vanity. His enemies said he was quick-tempered, intolerant, and suspicious. The fact is perhaps that he had been rather spoilt by home indulgence in his youth.

He was capable of deep affection, as the beautiful letters to his wife and children show, but that affection was mainly confined to his family circle. To the world at large he presented a cold, aloof demeanour, varied by sudden fits of temper. There was something febrile in his nature, as in Canning's, which was not altogether due to his wretched health. He was respected and feared, but not generally liked. It might have been said of him, as was said of an English statesman of our own day—he had not an enemy in the world, but he was cordially disliked by his many friends.

In politics he was not always a reliable colleague—which was a fault, but, as was shown by his friendship with Canning, he was no narrow party man—which we must count as a merit. He was a genuine reformer and compelled the Whigs to extend their reforming zeal to more vital things than the franchise. Here is his own statement of his creed: "I do not wish new institutions but to preserve and strengthen the old. Some would confine the advantages of those institutions to as small a class as possible, I would throw them open to all who have the ability to comprehend them and the vigour to protect them. Others again would annihilate them for the purpose of forming new ones on fanciful and un-tried principles. I would not only preserve them, but increase their efficiency and add to the number of their supporters." If he had been sitting in the British parliament to-day I fancy he would have allied himself with the younger Conservatives. In his own day he may be said to have lacked what Cavour called the *tact des choses possibles*. He was magnificent in gen-eralities but somewhat maladroit in tactics. But no one ever questioned his courage. The man who, sick and weary, undertook at short notice the mission to Canada had a very stout heart.

About his abilities it is hard to decide. He had a great gift of somewhat florid torrential oratory, but that is no uncommon thing. He had foresight, too, and imagination beyond most of his contemporaries. Indeed, in the decorous and somewhat drab circle of Whig statesmen he moved like a panther among polar bears. But it is not possible to put him, I think, in the first rank of nineteenth-century statesmanship, with Peel and Gladstone and Disraeli. There is a delightful story of his children once discussing whether their father's name in a hundred years' time would be mentioned in the history of England; and his son Charles, the "Master Lambton" of the picture, said, "I hope they will put it this way: 'In the reign of George IV lived the famous Mr. Lambton—he was a man of considerable talents.'" That is about the truth. He is famous, he will always be famous; but his talents were not more than considerable. The work he accomplished was greater than the man.

It is of that work I would speak. It is curious that all his years of laborious political agitation in England, his cabinet offices, his diplomatic successes, should be utterly forgotten, and that he should be remembered only by his few months in Canada. When Durham started on his mission Canada was virtually in revolution. The government, both in Lower and Upper Canada, had broken down, and the constitution was in fact suspended. England was comprehensively bored with the whole subject. Many believed that annexation by the United States was inevitable. Liberal English statesmen like Lord John Russell held that responsible

government for Canada meant a separation for good
and all, and that it would be better to separate at once
rather than attempt a foolish experiment. Tory statesmen like the Duke of Wellington declared, to quote
Wellington's words, that "local self-government and the
sovereignty of Great Britain were completely incompatible." With such a difficult background of home
opinion Durham began his work. He found French and
British in Quebec at bitter enmity, and the British in
Ontario torn by dissensions, and the United States very
ready to fish in troubled waters. He found, too, that
questions like the fate of the political prisoners and the
clergy reserves had complicated the real problem.

I need not remind you of the main lines of his *Report*.
Some of his work did not endure. The union of Upper
and Lower Canada, designed to provide an English
majority, led to a stalemate and had to be revised; but
it should be remembered that Durham regarded this as
only a temporary expedient, and looked forward always
to that scheme of federation which was to be realized in
the next thirty years. The foundation stone of his
structure was the gift of responsible government, and
that endured. The kernel of the *Report* is to be found
in the famous words, "The Crown must consent to
carry the government on by means of those in whom
the representative members have confidence." The old
gibe that Durham had little to do with the *Report*, that
it was conceived by Gibbon Wakefield, written by
Charles Buller, and only signed by Durham, has no
truth in it; the *Report*, it is clear, was Durham's own
from start to finish. There was nothing novel in the
doctrine. It was the creed of Burke and Fox, of Pitt
and Canning; it had long been the accepted British
policy. Durham's achievement lay in the fact that he

had the courage to give it a wider application, to shake off the dead hand of colonial office paternalism and to trust the Canadian people. I need not remind you that there may be as much originality in applying an accepted creed to novel conditions as in inventing a new one.

He returned, as I have said, to misunderstanding, abuse, criticism, and to death. He was not to see the fulfilment of his hopes. That had to be the task of Lord Elgin, the ablest, I think, of nineteenth-century viceroys, and of great Canadians like Robert Baldwin. Durham had ruined his own career by his work in Canada, but he had helped to build a nation. He made Britain proud of Canada, and Canada proud of Britain and of herself. I am no lover of what is too much the fashion to-day, what I might call "ideological intolerance," under which this or that system of government is declared to be the only absolute truth; a system of government which suits one country may be less suitable for another. But I believe that democracy in the widest sense must remain the creed of western civilisation, of the French, British, and American peoples, for it is consonant with something very deep in their tradition and spirit. Of that democracy, responsible government is the core and heart, and we do well to pay tribute to a man who sacrificed health and reputation in its cause.

The Civil Service[1]

I THINK I can claim to be one of you. I, too, have been at various times in my life a Civil Servant, in South Africa and in Britain. A temporary Civil Servant and not a regular member of the hierarchy; but enough of a Civil Servant to understand the value of your fine tradition.

Let me begin by saying something with which no one can disagree. A well-organised Civil Service is essential to the government of a civilised State. Just as a great business must possess a continuing machinery which is not dependent upon any one man, so a nation must possess an organisation to fulfil the daily tasks of government which is independent of the ups and downs of party strife. The Roman Empire as created by Augustus owed its success to the highly competent Civil Service which he established, and it was this Civil Service which remained for centuries the true cement of Rome.

A Civil Service is essential to any government, but it is especially necessary in a democracy. It is instructive to examine the steps by which constitutional government came into being in Britain. Under the Tudors the detailed work of administration was done by officials under the personal direction of the king. It was an expert service, and on the whole pretty efficient. But when the House of Commons asserted its authority in the seventeenth century there arose at once this difficulty. A popular assembly cannot admin-

[1]*Civil Service Dinner. Ottawa. 7th October, 1937.*

ister a State, and the problem was how to combine expert administration with a reasonable measure of popular control. Oliver Cromwell found the task impossible, and, being a practical man and knowing the meaning of efficiency, he came at once to loggerheads with his parliament. The problem was not solved until during the eighteenth century something in the nature of a permanent Civil Service was created.

A civilised nation, therefore, has to avoid two extremes. A too powerful Civil Service becomes a bureaucracy, as in the later Roman Empire, and a danger to individual freedom. A too weak Civil Service becomes a muddle, and confusion is just as dangerous to freedom as tyranny. Civilisation, therefore, demands an expert service which is popularly controlled.

What are the essentials of such a service? In the first place it must be open to all. It must offer a career to talents drawn from every class. It must not be the preserve of one social grade or a hunting-ground for political jobbery. The method adopted in Britain and elsewhere is a qualifying examination open to anyone. That, I believe, is the best system for general purposes, but in certain cases it may be well to vary it. The British Colonial Service, for example, which sends out young men to administer large districts in the tropical parts of the Empire, has dropped the examination method, and selects its people by an elaborate system of cross-bearings—reports from school and college, private advice, and personal interviews. That, I think is reasonable, for there is no guarantee that the young man who is a good mathematician or writes neat Latin verses, will be therefore a capable administrator of a wild piece of country.

But, by and large, for all ordinary purposes I think

the qualifying examination is the right method. It guarantees for one thing freedom from political bias. In a free country governments periodically change; but meantime the work of administration must be carried on, and it is vital that those who handle the day-to-day tasks should have no *parti pris* in their work. A Labour Government in England can look for just as loyal help from our Civil Service as any other form of government. It is the business of the Civil Service not to make policies, but to carry out the policies on which the people's representatives decide.

I would add another reason for this political independence which appeals especially to one who, like myself, was for many years a Member of Parliament. If a politician has no power to put men into the government service he will lead a much pleasanter life. His mail in the morning will not be congested with applications from constituents who want a job.

A second essential for a Civil Service is security of tenure. An official with expert knowledge, which increases daily, should know for certain that, so long as he does his work competently, he will be unaffected by the mutations of party government. What is called the "spoils to the victor" system spells ruin to any effective administration, and it is noteworthy that wherever this system exists to-day wise Governments are doing their best to get rid of it.

Again a Civil Service must be anonymous. It must be a silent service, as silent as the British navy is supposed to be. It does not advertise its work, or its views, or its members. To-day, when there is so much vulgar advertisement in the world, when politicians talk wildly about "ideologies"—horrid word!—it is a comfort to have a great service which knows its job, does it, and holds its tongue.

Above all, a Civil Service must attract the best talent among the youth of the State. The public service must be regarded as one of the most honourable of all pursuits. The financial rewards held out by it in Britain are trivial as compared with those of commercial and financial careers. But the prestige is enormous, and long may this continue. The service of the State has, in the eyes of the ordinary Englishman, a distinction of its own which outweighs the solemn fact that no one will make a fortune in it. I am glad to think that the same fine tradition governs the Civil Services on this side of the Atlantic.

THE MONARCHY AND THE COMMONWEALTH[1]

YOU have done me a great honour in admitting me to the fellowship of your University, and I offer you my sincerest gratitude. When I look at Bishop's, situated in this beautiful valley, as flowery and green as anything in England, I think of the phrase that Lord Falkland used when he brought his friends from Oxford to stay with him at his country house of Great Tew. He called it "a college situate in a clearer air". Lord Falkland was a famous Royalist in difficult days, and it occurred to me that I might speak to you to-day for a short time, not about myself and my office—that would be a dreary task—but about the sovereign whom I have the honour to represent. Our system of Government is a monarchy, an hereditary monarchy. Let us consider for a few minutes what exactly that means.

The British Commonwealth to-day is a community of free nations—The United Kingdom, Eire, Canada, Australia, New Zealand, South Africa—under one King. King George VI is King of Canada just as much as he is King of England. Now, though the Dominion of Canada is a comparatively new creation, monarchy in Canada is a very old one. The two great stocks in our population are the British and the French. Great Britain has never been anything but a monarchy—even the Commonwealth under Cromwell was a sort of monarchy and Cromwell was one of the greatest of our monarchs. There have been kings in Britain for fifteen centuries. The French in Canada, too, have never been

[1]*Bishop's College. Lennoxville. June, 1938.*

anything but monarchists. They came to Canada long before the French Republic was thought of. We may say, therefore, that Canada is not only a loyal nation, but a royalist nation.

Monarchy means the ultimate rule of one man. You may say that it is the universal system in the world to-day, though it takes different forms. In a republic it is elective and temporary. The President of the United States, for example, during his term of office is the chief executive officer, and in some ways the most powerful ruler in the world. In another type of republic, like that of France, the president's position, while one of dignity, is largely honorary, and the actual direction of the government belongs, as with us, to the Prime Minister. In Germany the Führer, and in Italy the Duce are the supreme executives. Their authority is elective only in the sense that the nation acquiesces in it, and it is indefinite in duration. An hereditary monarch like ours is wholly different. It is not elective; our king is monarch for life; and, while in law he is the supreme executive and the ultimate legislative authority, in practice he delegates his power to others, and has done so for several centuries. As the phrase goes, he "reigns" but does not "govern".

What does that mean? What exactly are King George's powers? They are hard to define, and one of the reasons for that is that they are so real and vital. Steadily during the last two centuries in Britain the Throne has lost its definable powers and gained in dignity and significance. In law the King can do no wrong. His Ministers alone are responsible and accountable. He cannot initiate a policy. What is done in his name is the work of others, and they get the credit or the blame. He never interferes, unless, as sometimes happens, things come to a deadlock and he is asked to intervene. His importance is not so much in what he does as in what he is. We are a democracy in which the will of the people prevails by means of their elected representatives. But the King represents the people in a deeper sense—the abiding continuity of the nation behind all the mutations and vicissitudes of parties.

Now I am not going to exalt our system above other systems and compare an hereditary monarchy to its advantage with a republic or a dictatorship. There is far too much of what you might call ideological intolerance abroad in the world to-day. The Fascist says that his system is the only right one, and the Communist makes the same claim for his. They have an almost fanatic missionary zeal and want to make the world conform to their creed. I do not say that about our system. I say that it is a good one, and that it suits us better than any other. There is one feature which differentiates it from all others. You can introduce a dictatorship or a republic and get it working at once. We have seen that happen with dictatorships in Russia and Germany and Italy, and in Portugal they have a new republic which seems to get along fairly well. But you cannot start *de novo* an hereditary monarchy such as ours. It is an organic thing and must be the slow work of time. Therefore, as something which grows, it is likely to have deeper roots and be more enduring than something which is merely put together.

How did it grow? Well, I am not going to give you a lecture on constitutional history, but I would remind you how long-descended our kingship is. The blood of

our royal house goes back before the Norman Conquest
to the old Saxon kings. There is no descent comparable
to it in duration in the world to-day; there never has
been, for compared to it other royal houses, like the
Claudo-Julian House in the Roman Empire, the Capets,
the Bourbons, the Hapsburgs, the Hohenzollerns, were
short-lived. More important, our monarchy has always
existed with the consent of the nation. It has never
been a tyranny imposed from above.

The British people have often treated their kings
cavalierly. In early days a man was king because he
was the principal landowner or the best leader in battle,
but in Britain he was never the master of the people
but always their servant. As conditions changed his
powers and functions have been revised, and that was
often a difficult business. The Tudors came into power
at a time when England was broken by plague and
civil war, and to get things straight they had to
establish a paternal government. With the Reformation and the change of economic conditions this paternalism became irksome, and because Charles I did
not realise it he lost his head. In the same way his son
James was sent packing because he desired government
to be according to his own wishes and not those of the
nation. So we discovered our modern system of parliamentary government and limited monarchy, which
on the whole has worked very well.

What I want you to realise is that even when we
thought very little of the monarch we always thought
highly of the monarchy. We might revise its functions,
but by that very revision we increased its prestige. In
the eighteenth century and the beginning of the nineteenth the popularity of the Georges sank very low, till

it reached bottom with George IV. But even when the character of the monarch was despised the office was immensely respected. Britain has rebelled quite often against kings, but never against kingship.

Why has kingship this peculiar prestige with us? Let me suggest one or two reasons.

In the first place it focuses the historic consciousness of the nation. It is the mystical, indivisible centre of national union. It is the point around which coheres the nation's sense of a continuing personality. It gives us of to-day a feeling of partnership with the old makers of Britain when we realise that they too served the Throne, and the same Throne. Let me take the analogy of a family. You know how in a family there is usually someone—the father—more often the mother—or perhaps an elder sister or an elder brother—who seems to bind the generations together. He or she is the linch-pin of the coach; when they die we have a sense not only of personal bereavement, but of family disintegration. That is the function which the King performs in our big family of nations, and when King George V used to call his people around the Christmas hearth and speak to them, we realised the enormous value of such a centre of memories and loyalties.

No nation can endure without something of the kind. That was where the City States of ancient Greece failed; they had no centre of conscious unity, no continuing link between past and present. Augustus, when he founded the Roman Empire, saw the need of something of the kind, and his solution was the state worship of "Roma et Augustus", the majesty of Rome combined with his own person, with what was called his "genius". If you have not a centre of historic national consciousness you have to invent one. For example, to-day in Italy they have exalted the ancient majesty of Rome; in Germany the Nordic tradition; in Russia the personality of the dead Lenin in his sarcophagus in the Moscow square. We are more happily situated, for we have not to invent. In our royal house we have a thread on which we can string all the stages in our development, all the ventures, the failures, and the triumphs of our long story.

In the second place the Throne is the centre of Empire unity. We are a Commonwealth and an Empire. A Commonwealth of free nations, monarchies of which King George is king, and one quasi-republic, Eire, which for external purposes and for defence is a kind of monarchy. We are also an Empire of territories directly governed by the Crown which are slowly moving towards responsible government. In all history there has been no such jumble of different and apparent inconsistent units in one polity. What is there in common between Canada, a white man's democracy, and, say, the Fiji Islands; or between India, which is now making its first trial of self-government, and Britain, which has been self-governing for a thousand years? What is there in common between peoples who represent every race-stock on earth? Yet these differences are differences within a unity. The Throne binds the whole Empire together and gives cohesion to a vast growth whose ultimate destiny is unpredictable. There are other binding influences, such as the bonds of sentiment and blood and of tradition, but without the unifying power of the Crown none of these would bind for long. You cannot do without the personal touch in human affairs, and it is the more important the lower you go in the scale of development. To millions of dark-skinned peoples in Asia and Africa and the isles of the sea government means the person of the Sovereign.

Again, a hereditary monarchy such as ours prevents any violent changes which weaken attachment. Amurath succeeds to Amurath as day to night and summer to spring. At every election of a new president of a republic there is bound to be strife and faction and unsettlement until the people settle down to business. When one dictator succeeds another there is apt to be something worse. In a hereditary monarchy there is nothing of the sort. We saw in the crisis of King Edward's abdication in December 1936 how smoothly and naturally our system works. The hereditary principle has, of course, its drawbacks, but as a practical method it has the enormous advantage that it is beyond popular caprice. It operates automatically and unconsciously like a process of nature, and therefore it has the strength of a natural process. A king who reigns, not by election or by a sudden popular impulse, but by long-established legal right, has a sanction behind him to which no transient dictator or president can attain.

There is one thing more important still about our monarchy. The Throne is outside class altogether—not only above it but wholly divorced from it. I am not one of those who believe in the classless society of which Karl Marx dreamed. I do not think that it is possible in the world as God made it, for if you abolished classes to-day you would have them forming again tomorrow. But it is a tremendous thing to have a head of the State for whom class has no meaning. The Throne is not only higher than any human estate, but it is of a different kind from any other. The monarch is akin to everybody in the realm; the superior of all, but also the friend of all. Everyone can call him brother with exactly the same title.

Consider how wonderful a thing it is that the man who is lifted up above the nation should also be the nation itself in its most typical form. In reverencing our King we reverence what is best in ourselves. A very great genius perhaps would break his heart on the British Throne, for he would have too little scope for action. What we ask for in a monarch is not a super-man—we leave that to dictatorships—but someone of like nature with ourselves, with the same tastes and traditions. Providence has been kind to us, for in recent years in King George V and King George VI we have been given kings with the qualities which the ordinary man throughout the Commonwealth can value. There is a famous sentence of Oliver Goldsmith's which on this point contains all the law and the prophets.—"The Englishman," he says, "is taught to love the king as his friend, but to acknowledge no other master than the laws which he himself has contributed to enact." The king is the friend of every citizen, but the master of none, for friendship implies a noble equality.

V

EDUCATION

SOME NOTES ON EDUCATION[1]

I AM very glad to have the chance of addressing an audience which is composed of those whom I regard as my colleagues. All my life I have had to do with educational questions. For a quarter of a century I was partner in a publishing house whose work lay very largely in educational literature, and for eight years I represented the Scottish universities in Parliament. Also as a Scotsman I hope I may claim a traditional interest in the subject, for ever since the days of John Knox, Scotland has set before herself a high educational ideal and to a large extent has realised it. I like the story of the visitor from the south who, looking over a wide expanse of bleak moor and bog, turned to a Highland shepherd beside him and said "In God's name, what does this country produce?" The shepherd solemnly removed his cap and said, "Sir, in God's name it produces educated men."

I welcome the chance of meeting you to-day, for all who are concerned in this great task should stand shoulder to shoulder. The difficulties of the teacher's profession do not decrease as time goes on. The Greeks had a proverb, "Whom the gods hate they make schoolmasters", and I daresay that some of you at times, in your work, have suspected this divine malevolence. Your business is with the things of the mind and the character. In a world desperately busied with making a livelihood these things are not always held at their proper value. The philistine regards with suspicion

[1]*Ontario Educational Association. Toronto. 29th March, 1937.*

105

the seeker after truth, and the materialist looks
askance at the idealist. The wares that we offer in the
market place are apt by the crowd to be disregarded,
or to be priced too low. The mind of the ordinary man
is inclined to be in a groove, with the result that there
is no lateral extension, and it cannot look beyond its
narrow interests. Moreover in that groove it has no
prospect ahead. I have heard more than one business
man declare that the single point he had to consider
in his work was profit, profitability. Well, if you define
profitability wisely and generously that may be a very
good slogan. But the man who, in his business, con-
siders only what is called in the terrible American
phrase, "experiential cash value", is no better than a
fool and he is moving fast towards that failure which
he will richly deserve.

You have another difficulty to face. National education must be highly organised, and there is always a
risk that, when you create an elaborate mechanism, the
machinery tends to be cherished for itself, so that its
ultimate purpose is forgotten. System you must have,
but, in any great service, system may come to be regarded as an end in itself, and worshipped for its own
sake. All of us, you and I, are apt at times to play with
counters rather than with realities. We seize upon some
detail, some specific reform, shall I say, and because it
fits readily into our scheme we give it an importance
that it does not deserve. The famous Cambridge
classical scholar and poet, the late A. E. Housman,
once criticised an Oxford colleague for his use of texts,
with that acerbity which unhappily appears in classical
scholarship, especially when the disputants belong to
different universities. "Mr. So-and-so," he said, "uses
texts much as a drunk man uses lamp-posts, not for the

purpose of illumination, but to correct his instability."
That is a comment, I think, that we might all take
to heart.

I confess I find it a little difficult to know what to
say to you to-day. There is no subject on which it is
more easy to talk loosely and platitudinously than
education. In the British House of Commons a few
years ago, having had to make many speeches on the
topic, I felt impelled to say that, having said all the
things about education that I knew to be true, and a
good many things that I knew to be untrue, I proposed
in the future to hold my tongue. I cannot talk to you
to-day about Canadian problems, for I am still in the
position of a learner. I hope I may have something
useful to say about them before I finish my term of
office here, but that time is not yet. I thought of
speaking to you about the teaching of history, for that
is a matter which lies very near my heart. I believe
that some understanding of the past is necessary before
we can understand the present or forecast the future.
I should like also to talk to you about the teaching of
English. It has always seemed to me that the first
thing education must do for any child is to teach him
to express his thoughts clearly and accurately in his
own language—a gift just as important for the business
man as for the politician and the writer. But these are
large topics and would take up more time than you can
give me. So to-day I would only offer you a few general
reflections which I am afraid will be of little value, for
I am sure that you will have thought of them for
yourselves.

We shall not differ, I think, about the aim of education. It can never be the mere acquisition of learning. There is an old saying of the two older English

universities that in the one they have read nothing and know everything, and in the other they have read everything and know nothing. I do not know which result is the more disastrous. I think that we often tend to exaggerate grossly the value of knowledge as such. The object in education is to train the mind, not to crowd the memory. It is not to manufacture ammunition wagons, receptacles for storing up material, which by itself is useless. It is to make guns with which to fire off the ammunition.

In Canada, the subject takes on a special character, which makes it a little different from the same subject at home. This is a land of wide distances; it is a land in which, over a large part, society is still in the making—a pioneer land. Therefore the eternal problem which faces us everywhere will, in your case, have special difficulties. That problem I should define as how to strike a just balance between the academic and the practical; how to combine education in the broadest sense, which is the training of the mind and character, with the acquisition of the special technique which enables a boy to earn his livelihood. I have said that the opposition is between the academic and the practical, but that is really a false distinction. All true education is practical, for it makes the mind a keener and truer weapon, tempers it, puts play and elasticity into it, so that it is better fitted for the practical tasks when they present themselves. So I should define the problem more narrowly. It is how to combine a reasonable modicum of general culture with what we call vocational training, the acquisition of that special knowledge which directly concerns the making of a livelihood.

Put broadly, the problem is how to combine human-

ism with technique. By humanism in education I mean
the study of man in all his relations, as thinker, as
artist, as a social and moral being; and by technique I
mean the study of what may be called brute fact.
Humanism is primarily a question of values. There is,
of course, a great deal of technique in all humane
studies. Take, for example, the study of the Latin and
Greek classics. There, apart from the literary and historical side, you find a crop of supplementary tech-
niques—palaeography, epigraphy, numismatics, archae-
ology and so forth. But the primary purpose of humane
studies is the understanding of human nature, the
broadening of the human interests and the better appreciation of the values of human life. Technique raises
none of these questions. It is the mastery of brute fact
for a definitely utilitarian purpose. Its concern is with
material things and not with those of the spirit.

Now let me confess that my sympathies are with
what Matthew Arnold called "the fine old fortifying
classical curriculum". The best education requires a
foundation of humane learning. By humane learning
I mean simply the disinterested pursuit of truth for its
own sake, apart from any incidental advantages. I
would define the humanities in the broadest sense.
They are not only art, literature, history, philosophy
and religion; they are each and every science, provided
it is pursued in a certain way. It is not the subject
matter which makes the distinction. You can give
humane value to any subject if you have the right
attitude of mind. Therefore, I am all in favour of
Universities like Oxford and Cambridge having nothing
to do with the narrower kind of vocational training.
When they teach law it should be the science of law,
not the practice, which a man will learn far better in a

lawyer's office. If they teach engineering it should be the science of engineering, and not the practical side, which is much better learned in a place like Glasgow or Sheffield. If they teach medicine it should be the science of medicine; the clinical side requires the great cities and the great hospitals. That is our old idea of higher education. Up to the age of twenty-one or so a young man should be engaged in humane learning and the mental training which is derived from it. After that he should acquire the special technique needed for whatever profession he chooses.

That is all very well, but it applies only to a particular kind of society. It applies either to the well-to-do, who can afford a leisurely training, or to a simple society like, shall I say, Quebec in the old days, when the learned professions were not over-crowded and there was very little demand for technological skill. "The temper of our age is too desperate for this elegant individualism. Because the social structure is shaken men demand of every intellectual activity that it shall serve, directly or indirectly, some recognisable social need." That is a quotation from the recent inaugural address delivered by the new Professor of Greek at Oxford, and it is profoundly true. The leisurely old-fashioned conception, which I have tried to define, certainly does not apply to Canada as we know it to-day. What we are concerned with in education is to enable youth of every class, including the poorest, to earn an honest living; and at the same time to equip a boy for his life's work; to give him some background of education which will provide him with a wise perspective and a fund of unutilitarian interests, and incidentally fit him to be a good citizen.

I have stated the problem. Far be it from me to

attempt to suggest a solution. We must face it with commonsense and a proper perception of realities. It is no good giving a boy a smattering of culture if he is going to starve, and it is not much more good to provide him with some equipment for earning his daily bread and to leave his mind narrow and inelastic. I am very certain that you have both duties well in view. I have been much cheered lately in visiting various technical and commercial schools in Ontario, to find that an honest endeavour was made throughout the technical training to preserve an element of what I call the humanities. That is one side to a solution. The other may be found in the way in which the technical training itself is conducted. If it is regarded not merely as the acquisition of a certain number of rules of thumb, but as a piece of serious mental training, then you are introducing the spirit of the humanities into the vocational side. You are producing not only technicians, but men and women with minds. You are producing potential citizens.

Canadian conditions raise another problem. From the nature of things your educational organisation should be a more elastic thing than that which we have in an old country like Britain. If we are to have an educated people in the true sense we must not only have schools organised without pedantry and with a due sense of realities, but we must be prepared to go beyond the schools. The work of an institution like your Frontier College points the way. Many Canadians cannot take advantage of our educational system, and in any case the true education for many boys only begins after they leave school. The question of adult education has a special importance in a land like ours. I have been connected with the Workers' Educational

Association at home almost since its start. It has now become a great organisation, and in my opinion it is one of the most valuable things in English life. It enables young men, who have had very few educational chances, to acquire a knowledge and skill which is of direct practical value in their trade. That is one side, and a very valuable one. But the most impressive aspect of it is the cultural, which is followed with no idea of an immediate practical advantage. I remember finding in a manufacturing town a class composed of young workers in the steel trade. What do you think they were studying? Plato. Perhaps they had not much Greek, but they had uncommonly alert minds, and they were tackling the business with extraordinary enthusiasm and intelligence. And I remember that once, at the request of their Trade Union, I acted as examiner for a prize which was given for essays by working miners in Nottinghamshire. Most of these had been to W.E.A. classes, and I can only say that the result filled me with amazement. The essay on Shakespeare, which won the prize, was written by a working miner of twenty-one, and was one of the best pieces of literary criticism I have ever read.

I offer you in all humility these few reflections on a subject which you understand far better than I do. I have only one last word to say to you, and that is about the importance of your task. In a large part of Canada your duties are those of the pioneer. You have to face many of the hardships and the hazards of pioneering. In my tours through the drought areas of the Prairies last fall, I acquired a deep respect for your profession, for I found many teachers on slender salaries gallantly fulfilling their duties, and sharing to the full in the discomforts of the depression. We praise, and readily praise, the fortitude of the Prairie farmers; let us not forget the fortitude of the Prairie teachers.

As for your profession in general, I do not think it possible to exaggerate its value. You are to-day in the position which the clergy held in the Middle Ages. You have in your power the making of the soul of a people. Your business is to create citizens in the fullest sense of the word. In the long run you are far more important than any other instrument of popular instruction, more than the press or the cinema or the radio. Therefore, I want to see every teacher glorify his profession. He cannot hold his head too high. He cannot make too exalted claims for his work. We have to see to it that the profession is made such that it will attract the best men, and that it will offer a career which gives full opportunity for every quality of head and of heart. It is a great task in which you are engaged, and, as a humble worker in the same field, I would bid you Godspeed.

The Interdependence of Knowledge[1]

IT IS a privilege to be with you to-day, if only to have had the chance of listening to Mr. Henry Clay's address—I wish I had been able to hear also Mr. Warren and Mr. Wolman. You have done me a great honour in asking me to deliver a kind of epilogue to these lectures. But please do not misunderstand me. My studies have not lain for the most part in the spheres to which they have directed your attention, so I cannot speak as an expert. But I have had something to do with the practical business of government in various parts of the globe, so in my few words to you I am going to speak as the average citizen, the plain man, what philosophers call the "ordinary consciousness", that ordinary consciousness which is the raw material of philosophy, and which provides philosophers with their following.

I like the title of the series, "The State *in* Society", for it admits the important truth that the community is an organisation greater than the State—a truth too often forgotten to-day. One purpose, I gather, is to reach a more intelligent understanding of the group of sciences which we call Sociology and to view them in the right perspective. I have seen Sociology described as in a special sense *the* American science, and certainly much brilliant work has been done on this side of the Atlantic. I remember also some uncomplimentary observations of M. Bergson, who denied that it was a science at all. How do we define a science? Shall we

[1]*McGill University. Montreal. 10th February, 1939.*

114

say something like this:— a science is a body of true
assertions, and these assertions are logically and sys-
tematically inter-connected? Do the so-called social
sciences fulfil these conditions? The first undoubtedly:
a vast body of more or less accurate data has been
assembled. The second—that these data are sys-
tematically inter-connected? Well, I am not so sure.

Do you remember a sentence in an early philosophical
work of the late Lord Balfour where he wrote, "The
science of Sociology has been planned out by some very
able philosophers much as a prospective watering place
is planned out by a speculative builder." You observe
the underlying sarcasm, the touch of *esprit malin*.
But personally I see nothing wrong in the definition;
my only complaint is that the town-planning of the
social sciences has not been more carefully and thoroughly done. For the study of man as a social being
has many ramifications and involves many branches of
knowledge. There is the historical and geographical
background; there is the embryology of the State; there
is the study of developed relations—the sciences of
economics, of law, of the technique of government;
there is the ethical side; and there is the ultimate
question of purpose which involves political philosophy.
None of these can be completely isolated. The student
of any one of them must at any rate be aware of the
others, and must have his windows open to a wide
landscape. Therefore, more than in most branches of
knowledge, we need a related and balanced order of
studies.

It is to foster this purpose that these lectures have
been arranged. The pursuit of any one branch in
isolation may have no educative value at all. I have
known people who had the whole jargon of classical

economics at their fingers' ends; I have known people
who could reel off every theory of the State that was
ever devised; but in neither case had their minds received any serious education. They would have been
better employed in the study of a thing like heraldry—
which at any rate is picturesque. There is a good deal
of talk to-day of autarky, *autarkeia*, self-sufficiency—all
of it dangerous; but there is nothing more dangerous
than this intellectual autarky, this artificial isolation of
branches of thought, the value of which lies in their
organic interconnection.

In the few minutes granted to me let me summarise
very briefly the dangers of this isolationism.

The first is intellectual barrenness. If you have a
closed system of thought there is no chance of development. Your subject is never fertilised by contact with
the real world. What should be regarded as a means is
taken as an end. If I may borrow a metaphor from Mr.
Justice Cardozo, late of the Supreme Court of the
United States, "The inn that shelters for the night is
not the journey's end. The traveller must be ready for
the morrow." You can see this danger in political
science, where a comparison and classification of constitutions can be the most arid of studies. You find it
in economics. You find it in law, which, in the hands of
certain judges and jurists, is merely a game of permuta-
tions and combinations played with a limited number
of dogmatic counters. These dogmatists may declare
that that is the only way to keep the law stable; but
stability is not the same thing as stagnation.

A second danger of isolationism is that, lacking the
impulse to compare derived from cognate studies, we
can accumulate a mass of facts without any adequate

interpretation or evaluation. That is already too true of certain social studies, where we have got together the materials for a huge meal which we have not cooked and therefore will not be able to digest.

A third danger is that we fall into a vice which is too common to-day, and which we may call ideological intolerance. For consider. If I adopt certain views, legal, political or economic, in isolation, without understanding their historical background, I shall tend to take them for absolute truths, valid everywhere and at any time, and therefore excommunicate all who do not accept them.

Finally—and I speak with feeling as a lover of the English language—isolationism leads to the most abominable jargon. Have you ever considered how the standard of scientific writing has fallen in recent years? How few scientists can write English as Darwin wrote it, or Huxley! The reason is that, if you shut yourself up in a subject, you are apt to invent a shorthand in which you can communicate with other people interned in the same mausoleum. It saves trouble. Now a technical language, a reasonable system of symbols, is doubtless necessary, but we must remember that such symbols must expedite and not hinder, must clarify and not obscure knowledge. They are the means to an end, and that end is the student's understanding. But it is fatally easy to fall from a rational technical terminology into a barren isolationist jargon. I remember once hearing Lord Rutherford, one of the greatest men ever associated with this university, say that no conclusion in physics which he ever reached was of any use to him until he could put it into plain English. The mathematical formulae could follow, but he was not satisfied that his doctrine was sound unless he could put it into language understood by the ordinary man.

For these reasons, gentlemen, I think this series of lectures of the first importance, and I hope that the spirit which has inspired them will flourish among you. If it does it will be a god-send to McGill, to Canada, and to the world, for there is no truth which should be more often emphasised to-day than the interdependence of knowledge. Let us hope that the famous lines of Pope will some day become true—

"Physic of Metaphysic begs defence,
And Metaphysic calls for aid on Sense."

VI

YOUTH

A University's Bequest to Youth[1]

M Y TOAST is the Victoria University, which to-day
is celebrating a century of active and beneficent
life. Its history is a vital part of the history of the
Province of Ontario and of the Dominion of Canada.
Its foundation was one of the many great achievements
of the Methodist Church and of those United Empire
Loyalists who played so large a part in the building of
the Canadian nation. I have been reading with profound interest the late Dr. Burwash's history of this
University, in which the development of an educational
institution is traced against the background of the
development of Canada. It is a story of which you
may well be proud, and I, as one of your youngest
graduates, can share in that pride.

On such an occasion we rightly allow our minds to
dwell upon the past that we may gain hope and confidence from the recollection of difficulties surmounted
and duties accomplished. But to-night I would rather
direct your thoughts to the present and to the future.
There is a letter of Mr. Gladstone's to Lord Acton in
the last years of his life in which he wrote: "The world
of to-day is not the world in which I was bred and
trained and have principally lived. It is a world which
I have much difficulty in keeping on terms with."
These are melancholy words. No man or institution
can live on the past if they desire to endure. If they
lose touch with their age it means that they have lived
too long. A University such as this, which looks for-

[1] *Victoria University Centenary. Toronto. 10th October, 1936.*

121

ward to a long career of usefulness, can never afford
for one moment to get out of terms with the present.
Its task is to interpret that present as a bequest to the
future. Therefore to-night, in offering you the toast of
Victoria University, I would ask you to look at the
world not as it has been, but as it is and as it may be.

The minds of men fall naturally into two types.
There are those who love novelties for their own sake,
and like the ancient Athenians are always seeking after
a new thing. There is the other type which adheres to
old things—again for their own sake. That means two
different kinds of bias. The wise and balanced mind
will of course like neither the old nor the new for its
own sake, but will consider their essential value. But
few of us reason soberly, for at heart we are all senti-
mentalists. Now each bias has its danger. The novelty-
loving mind runs a risk of being blown about by every
wind of doctrine and losing its roots. The other mind
is in danger of sticking fast in a groove and losing any
power of development.

The danger Mr. Gladstone spoke of belongs to the
second type. His was what we may call the conservative mind, spelling the word, of course, with a small *c*.
That is my own danger, if I may make a confession.
So far as my inclinations are concerned I frankly prefer
the old-fashioned world of my boyhood. I am disposed
to agree with what a friend of mine is never tired of
declaring, that the horse is the basis of civilisation, that
the speed of a horse is the maximum speed for a
civilised man, and that anything beyond that is barbarism. In moments of exasperation I sometimes feel
that civilisation's worst enemy was the man, or the
men, who invented the internal combustion engine. I
have little admiration for the Mr. Brisks and the Mr.

Talkatives who exult childishly over every little im-
provement in our material apparatus.   I sometimes
have a fear that human happiness, and even human
comfort, have not been greatly improved by scientific
progress, and that my grandfather, who jogged about
on an old horse and who was concerned simply with the
affairs of his parish, had a better kind of life.

I think many of us must at times fall into that mood.
It is sentiment of course, not reason, and it is a dangerous sentiment which must be resisted unless we are to
suffer Mr. Gladstone's misfortune.   It is never any use
to kick against the pricks.   So, when these sad moods
of reminiscence come over us, the right cure, I think, is,
in the old-fashioned Scots phrase, "to count our
mercies." We must attain some kind of viewpoint and
get a proper perspective.   Let us cast our minds back
and consider how much gain there is in the last quarter
of a century to balance the loss.

Look back to the years before the Great War.   Our
first thought about them is that in the retrospect they
seem a time of unbelievable ease and prosperity. Yes,
but if we probe into our memory we shall find that they
were uncomfortable years. The world was arrogant and
self-satisfied, but behind all its confidence there was an
uneasy sense of impending disaster. The old creeds,
both religious and political, were largely in process of
dissolution, but we did not realise the fact, and therefore
did not look for new foundations. Well, the War, with
its abysmal suffering and destruction, did achieve one
thing. It revealed us to ourselves. It revealed how
thin the crust was between a complex civilisation and
primeval anarchy. If I were asked to name any one
clear gain from the War—and here I am speaking
of our own people—I would say that it was a new

humility. We had our pride shattered, and without humility there can be no humanity.

Since the War we have been trying to build up a new shelter from the weather, and it has not been an easy task. We have had to reject prejudices, and it has been like the plucking up of mandrakes. But at the same time I think we of the British Commonwealth have recognised that the foundations which our fathers laid are sound, and that it is only the superstructure which has to be altered. The generation behind us is a period of loss and gain—tragic loss, but also, I think, of indubitable gain. Let me put to you some of our gains. A great storm destroys much that is precious, but it may also clear the air and blow down trees which have been obscuring the view and making our life stuffy, and reveal in our estate possibilities of development which we had not thought of.

The first gain I would select is the *intellectual* gain. To-day we have fewer dogmas, but I think we have stronger principles. By a dogma I mean a deduction from facts which is only valid under certain conditions, and which becomes untrue if these conditions change. By a principle I mean something which is an eternal and universal truth. Take, for example, democracy. In the last century we were inclined to define it too absolutely, and to regard our British form of popular government as valid for all times and circumstances. To-day we see that these forms may require to be modified. But at the same time the great democratic principle, that government must be based upon individual liberty and self-discipline, is truer to-day than ever. We have learned, I think, that we must constantly overhaul our stock of political ideas and reject what is ossified and out of date, for it is only by such recensions that the enduring truths are seen in their true perspective.

After the intellectual gain comes the *social* gain. In the last twenty-five years we have seen the breakdown of many meaningless class barriers, and the uprooting of a great deal of false gentility. Knowledge, through an improved system of education and through many new channels, has been spread in a wider commonalty. Classes now are not in such water-tight compartments, but each understands more fully how the others live. With that understanding has come a livelier sympathy. How different, for example, is the attitude of better-off people now to the unemployment problem, compared with what it would have been in the pre-War years! We recognise more of a personal responsibility for the misfortunes of others. We feel the nation to be an organic thing, with the interests of all classes closely knit together. We realise that if one part is diseased the other parts cannot be in health.

In the narrower sense too, there is the *political* gain. To-day we have in the nations of our Commonwealth a closer integration. The State is not regarded as an aloof and impersonal thing; but as the whole people so organised that the powers of the community can be used, if necessary, to succour any part which is in distress. We have not lost that individual freedom which is the traditional basis of our national life, but we realise that freedom depends upon the acceptance of discipline. We are coming to see that the true meaning of civilised society is the free effort of individuals for ends which are also the ends of all.

Above all there is the *moral* gain, which I should describe as a wider humanity. Our sufferings have taught us that no nation is sufficient unto itself, and that our prosperity depends in the long run not upon the failure of our neighbours, but upon their success. The late King George, after his illness six years ago, spoke some wise words to his people. "I cannot dwell upon the generous sympathy," he said, "shown to me by unknown friends in many other countries, without a new and moving hope. I long to believe it possible that experiences such as mine may soon appear no longer exceptional; when the national anxieties of all the peoples of the world shall be felt as a common source of human sympathy and a common claim on human friendship." We may still be far from realising that hope, but I believe that we are on the road to it. Again I speak of our own people; and I cannot but feel that the fact that in recent years we have realised that the tasks we were facing were also the tasks of other nations, and that the dangers we were repelling were common to all the world, has done much to weaken what used to be our besetting sins, chauvinism and racial pride. We know more about other peoples, and that knowledge has brought a sympathy not only of the head but of the heart. Such a patriotism of humanity (which is in no way inconsistent with national patriotism) is the only ultimate foundation for international peace.

If I am right in my survey then we have a philosophy of life, a philosophy based upon a humble and reasoned optimism. A University's first business is to be the guardian of the central wisdom of humankind, a trustee of humane learning. It is therefore the duty of a University to transmit to the next generation a philosophy, the philosophy which we have learned from our fathers, widened and deepened by our own experience. That is our prime responsibility towards our youth, and that is why we must keep in touch with our own age. We dare not permit the next generation to be spiritually isolated from our own. We must look out upon the future without fear. Many of our young men to-day are tempted by creeds like Communism and Fascism, and why? Simply because they are clear-cut and confident things, and in the current confusion they long for something firm which they can lay hold of. We must be not less positive and confident.

What bequest can a University such as this make to the youth of the future? Not a detailed creed; that they must work out for themselves, for it will be conditioned by a thousand facts of which we have no knowledge. But an outlook, an attitude towards life. Its basis, as I have suggested, should be a reasoned optimism. How further shall we define it? As I see it, it should be an attitude which is reverent towards eternal things, and keen, practical and realistic towards temporal things. We may call it Humanism if we are allowed to define the term. Humanism does not mean that we take man as the measure of all things and make our only criterion his transient mundane interests. Its true purport is that we set as our first aim the freedom and integrity of the human spirit. That involves in my belief a spiritual religion. To-day you have done me the honour to make me a Doctor of Divinity, and I may speak for one moment as if I had the gown of a preacher on my shoulders. What has exalted our conception of humanity far beyond anything dreamed of by the philosophers of Greece and Rome? It is the Christian doctrine of the Incarnation. It is the fact that for nineteen centuries men have believed that for their sake the Word became flesh, and that the Eternal took upon Himself our mortality. It is the Christian religion which gives us our warrant for that lofty valuation of the human soul which is the meaning of humanism.

To-day we are confronted with a paradox. Multitudes of men are discarding the Christian faith and, indeed, all religion in the sense in which we commonly use the word. But religion is an ineradicable instinct of human nature. Man must find something to worship; when Israel disowned Jehovah it turned to Baal and Ashtaroth. Therefore, having cut loose from the creeds of their fathers, they must invent new worships of their own. They deify the work of their own hands—a State, a Leader, a Machine. They sanctify their whimsies and abase themselves in the dust before them. What is the consequence? A lack of critical and realistic power in connection with those idols which in the long run will shatter them. You cannot give to temporal things the reverence which should be confined to eternal things without making these temporal things a confusion and a laughing-stock.

This then, as I see it, should be the principle of that philosophy which we offer to youth—on the one side reverence and godly fear; on the other a cool, sane and clear-sighted attitude to the world around us. It is the latter with which I am specially concerned to-night. Our practical philosophy must be wholly undevotional. It should, as I see it, be both critical and dogmatic. We must remember that we live in a world where life must be conducted according to rules. We must be critical, but we dare not carry the critical dissolvent too far. We must have a house to shelter us. Civilisation after all is a kind of conspiracy. We need certain working conventions and, while these conventions must be jealously scrutinised, some rules, some conventions we must have if we are not to return to the primeval

mire. We cannot always be pulling down things before
we have discovered a substitute. In the ideal Commonwealth of Plato the philosopher was to be king, not the
sophist.

We have been passing through some years of sceptical
disillusion, but I think that that mood is vanishing, for
mere clever disintegration is ceasing to amuse. The
hope of the world lies in its critically constructive minds.
To-day law and government have no more the august
religious sanctions that they used to have. Among
sober-minded nations like our own they are hedged
about with no divinity; they are not taken for granted;
they have to justify themselves like every other human
creation. They are seen to be only the work of men's
hands. But more than ever we realise their urgent importance. We have come back to the old doctrines of
law and liberty from a different angle. Law has not
come down from Sinai; liberty is not an inalienable
natural right. Both are human constructions; but both
are recognised to be as vital to the peace and prosperity
of mankind as if they had been announced by the
trumpets of archangels.

That, gentlemen, I suggest as the key-note of the
practical humanism which I believe should be the attitude of a University, which is our deduction from a
stern experience, and which we can honestly commend
to those who come after us. It is based, as all true
humanism must be, upon the dignity given to man by
the love and fatherhood of God. It is resolute to keep
the things of God separate from the things which per-
tain to Caesar, and in Caesar's province to use the right
of untrammelled and ruthless criticism, since it is on
such terms that we set Caesar on his throne. We do
not deify our creations; we handle them like sensible

folk, making sure that they fulfil their purpose, re-modelling them when necessary, respecting them for their homely utility. We have seen the mischief which arises from heady dreams and the deification of human whimsies and human arrogance. We seek instead to be modest, sagacious, cool, critical, and, above all, sane, for only such a spirit can heal the fevers of the world.

There is a prayer used in my own Church of Scotland before the opening of Parliament which runs something like this: "Bless O Lord the two Houses of Parliament now assembled and over-rule their deliberations for the people's good." Over-rule, mark you, not guide or direct, the assumption being that they are almost certain to be wrong. I would take these words as a parable, for they might well be our attitude towards life and that law and government without which life cannot be lived. We dare not over-value authority since we know that it is our own creation, but we dare not under-value it, because we realise its supreme practical need. So we obey it—and we pray for it.

BOY SCOUTS

1[1]

I NEED not tell you I am deeply honoured to be
Chief Scout for Canada. I have known this movement since the very beginning. I knew Lord Baden-
Powell in the old days of the South African War, before
he had that inspiration of genius—one of the few real
inspirations of our time—which led to the great work
of his life. I have seen the beneficent work of the
Scouts at home and in many other countries; and now
I am proud to be associated with their work in Canada.
Here we have many great assets, but our chief asset is
our youth.

These are difficult days for all of us, when so many
old things have crumbled, when so many new problems
confront us which cannot be solved by the old maxims.
It is a bad time for middle-aged people who are set in
their ways. It is a difficult time for the timid. It is a
horrible time for the dogmatist. But it is a wonderful
time for youth. There has never been an age when
youth mattered more, when there were so many questions which only the vitality of youth could solve, when
the horizons were so wide for youth to travel to.

Just after the War I confess I was a little nervous
about our young people at home. Those who were at
school in the years before the Armistice seemed to
suffer from war-weariness more than those who had
fought at the front. They seemed to want only the
soft option, and to be interested only in the short game,

[1]*Boy Scouts' Association Dinner. Montreal. 1st May, 1936.*

131

to seek a secure niche where they could be comfortable and amuse themselves. That period did not last long. For many years I have had a good deal to do with British youth in the schools and the colleges, and I do not believe that the young entry were ever better than they are to-day. Their point of view seems to be that we live in a critical time, and that there must be no difficulty or danger which they are unable to face up to. They realise that the very foundations of society have been shaken, and that it is their business to make them solid again. Therefore, both physically and morally and mentally, they are adventurous. In their holidays they do not want to go to the ordinary seaside resort, and potter about with tennis racquet or golf clubs. They prefer something much more enterprising, such as looking after a batch of young Welsh miners on the land, or going as deck hands on a trawler to the Arctic. And another fine trait about them is that they seem to have lost all foolish class feeling. They will make friends with anybody and meet everyone on the basis of a common humanity. No, gentlemen, there is nothing wrong with our youth to-day.

Therefore it seems to me that the Scout movement has an importance which it has never had before. It has become a great school of national training for every class, and especially for the classes who do not as a matter of course follow the ordinary routine of school and college. It can give to the unprivileged all the benefits of the privileged.

In the first place it can give them discipline, without which no human being is quite happy. Man's natural lot is to be in a service with the ritual and discipline of a service—a free service, for he accepts the obligation of his own free will. It is a complete mistake to imagine that anyone is a natural anarchist, or is really happy in a slack society. For happiness we all need some kind of ritual and discipline provided it is accepted by us voluntarily, as free men.

In the second place scouting gives companionship. Fortunate people get their companionship through life from the associations of school and college. But the less fortunate are apt to fall into a kind of derelict individualism, which is neither pleasant nor useful. The danger is that, since companionship is essential, they will drift into the wrong kind of companionship. There is nothing worse for youth than loneliness. I have come across many cases of mischievous gangs of hobble-de-hoys in our cities at home which owed their existence to a perfectly honest and natural craving of young people for society. This instinct ill-directed may be a social scourge. If well directed it may be a powerful force of social stability.

Then again, the Scout movement for hundreds and thousands of boys has developed new interests in life. A boy brought up in a city slum is given access to the world of wild nature, of which he would otherwise know nothing. His sense of adventure is satisfied. The world suddenly becomes for him enormously wider and more amusing. In the same way, boys in remote rural areas are also given a glimpse of a wider world, and brought into the common fellowship of youth. All boys dream dreams and scouting is simply a boy's dream come true. That is the true genius and inspiration of the movement. It has married the aspirations and fancies of youth to the wider issues of life.

Most important of all, it gives them a code of conduct, something to live up to. In these days when there is a good deal of moral anarchy about, it is surely of the highest value that our youth should have something firm to hold to, some honourable standard to live by. The Scout movement stands firm upon certain great moral principles which no sophistry can undermine, for they are the basis of civilisation. It teaches the personal duties of courage and self-discipline and patience, and the social duties of sacrifice and sympathy. It holds before youth a nobler standard than mere worldly success. The movement is bound to no one religious sect or creed, but it stands for the eternal values which are at the base of all religion.

Scouting gets the full value out of youth by training it without blunting the edge of its spirit. You remember Disraeli's saying, "It is a great thing to be young; to be young and to be wise is to be irresistible." In Canada we of the movement are happily situated. We have not got to seek wild nature by ingenious methods. Here at our doors, close even to our greatest cities, is a vast and most varied country full of wild life, with huge territories still not fully explored, with frontiers not yet crossed. At home in Britain, to keep in touch with unspoilt nature, we may have to travel far, but here we need only cross the road. Canadian boys are always hearing of new discoveries and strange adventures, all within the boundaries of their own land. They can never get out of touch with Mother Earth. They need never complain of narrow horizons, for the horizon of Canada is always shifting. They have a great country still in the making, and they are called upon to share in that task.

That means, in a very special sense, that the ritual and discipline of Scouting is a direct and most practical preparation for their future careers. Since I have come to Canada I have tried to see as much as possible of

your youth, and, if I may say so, I have been deeply
impressed by its quality. If the opportunities before
it are great, it is the kind of breed that will rise to its
opportunities. And we older people associated with the
movement may well be conscious of *our* privileges. I
do not care how long a man may live; in one sense he
should never grow old. If we get out of touch with our
world we cease to be any use in it, and I have always
believed that the best way of keeping abreast of our
times is to keep in touch with youth.

Boy Scouts

2[1]

LAST year we had to announce certain changes in our organisation, and this year we can see the fruit of them. We have made admirable progress, for we have substantially increased the number of Scouts, we have very largely increased the number of Scout leaders, and we can show a remarkable increase in the number of training certificates. We are well on the way towards that membership of 100,000 which has long been our aim, and which I hope to see realised before my term of office in Canada is finished.

I have now been rather more than a year Chief Scout for Canada. I have travelled a good deal up and down the country between the Atlantic and the Pacific, and I hope before I have finished to go to both the eastern and the western Arctic, and to visit every province more at my leisure. I feel that I have only touched the margin of this great land, but I am determined before I leave it, really to get to know something about it. I am not sure that I won't end by knowing more about it than most Canadians.

Meantime let me record a few impressions gained during my travels. My first is the immense resources of the Dominion, resources so rich and varied that it would not be easy, I think, to find their parallel elsewhere in the world. We have only begun to scrape the edge of our inheritance. I am speaking of material assets, but even greater, I think, are the human assets,

[1]*Boy Scouts' Association Dinner. Montreal. 27th February, 1937.*

the character of the people. I have not often admired any human quality more than the fortitude and hopefulness of the men and women in the drought areas of the Prairies. But my strongest impression of all, I think, is of Canadian youth. Wherever I went, both in town and country, it seemed to me that I saw hordes of good-looking, healthy, vigorous children. Even in the stricken areas the children looked well, which meant that their parents were sacrificing a good deal to their welfare. That is a great thing. No doubt there is still much to be done in the way of health services and education, but at any rate you are giving the youngest generation a magnificent chance.

I have seen, too, a good deal of the older boys and girls, the material on which our movement draws. About them I want to say several things. In the first place there is a real, widely diffused desire for physical fitness. That, of course, is instigated and fostered by the older people, but it also represents a genuine instinct in youth. All these young people want, as they say, to "get into shape". Again, I have been struck with the way in which even town boys keep in touch with wild nature. Your admirable summer camps teach the lore of the bush; they harden and toughen the campers and introduce them to many of those crafts which are as old as human society. It is a spirit which I should like to see universal in the Empire. Again, I have been struck by what I would call the disinterested curiosity of your young people. They really want to know about things, and they are full of zest for living. There is no kind of decadence about them. They turn clear, candid questioning eyes towards the future. Lastly, I would praise their good-comradeship. They are excellent mixers. They do not pass a stranger by on the other side of the road; they want to know all about him and get into touch with him. At the first there may be a scrap; but—well—a scrap is not a bad form of introduction.

If I am right in my view it means that we have here all the materials in ample measure for our Scout movement. There is no country in the world where scouting should have more success. The purpose of scouting is to organise all these fine natural instincts—not to over-organise them, as they seem to be doing in Germany and in Italy, but to provide channels where they can have full play, and that reasonable discipline which is needed by all human effort.

I would offer you in all modesty one or two reflections drawn from my year of experience. The first and cardinal aim of the Scout movement is to foster the community spirit. Now the community spirit is deep in a boy's nature. Every boy is by nature a gangster in the best sense of that word. He has to get together with other boys properly to enjoy himself. But these gangs should not be too exclusive or too bellicose. I well remember in my own boyhood how we organised ourselves into little troops which, like Highland clans, were perpetually on the war-path. If another tribe were too strong for fisticuffs we fought them at a distance with bows and arrows. Now what Scouting does is to make the gang a fine and generous thing, where the principle is not exclusion but inclusion, and where the motive is not combat but comradeship. That means that our movement is a true democracy. The key-note of democracy, remember, is not mere freedom, though that is important. It is far more that higher freedom which comes from the sense of brotherhood.

My second reflection is the enormous value of this

Scout training in what, I fear, is a primary duty of
every nation to-day, the ability to defend itself. I do
not mean that I want to see our movement infected
with the poison of militarism. The less Scouting imi-
tates soldiering the better. But if it should ever be
necessary, in the words of our national song, "to stand
on guard for Canada", what better foundation could
you have than this sense of brotherhood, this feeling of
partnership, this love and devotion for our native land?
The real power of defence does not lie in accumulations
of war material, or even in the most perfect military
system. In the last resort it depends upon the quality,
the courage and fortitude of the people.

Again, Scouting is a counteractive to one of the
greatest dangers of modern life. The discoveries of
science and the advance in the material apparatus of
life have tended to mechanise society, to make everyone
a cog in a great impersonal machine. But human
society can never be mechanised, and, if you try, it will
cease to be human and cease to be a society. Scouting
cultivates the individual and the personality. It em-
phasises initiative and encourages self-development.
Moreover, it brings boys from town and country into
close touch with that wild nature which can never be
mechanised. I believe that on us, the free democracies,
there lies the special duty of insisting upon the immense
importance of personality, for, in many countries in the
world this seems to be forgotten. And there is no better
agent in this task than the movement with which we
are connected.

I would offer you one last reflection. It is a platitude
that the most vital thing in a country is its youth—a
platitude but also a fact, for even a truism is sometimes
true. That applies especially in the case of a land like

Canada, where your development has only begun, and where your future depends very largely upon the brains and character of your young men. You have questions to solve which require the enterprise and courage of youth, and in your development you have to face new scientific problems which require the best brains of youth. There never was a land in which young men needed a keener edge to their spirit. Canada is like the sleeping princess in the old nursery story; before she can be awakened the young prince must cut his way through the dark forest to reach the enchanted palace. Every Canadian boy is like the younger son in the fairytale. He starts off with his mother's blessing and his lunch in his pocket, and not much else. He knows there are all kinds of dragons and giants and enchantments to be vanquished, but he knows, too, that there are tremendous rewards for a quick brain and a stout heart. Can you offer anything better to youth than such a wide horizon?

BOY SCOUTS

3[1]

THIS is the third time since I came to Canada that I have had the honour to attend your annual dinner. I need not tell you that I find it one of the pleasantest occasions in the year. It gives me an opportunity of meeting many friends, and it gives me a chance of getting a bird's-eye view of our progress. Although I am always on the road and meeting Scouts everywhere, it is only on this occasion that I can get our work into proper perspective.

There are two things I want to say to you this evening. We are accustomed to repeat—I repeat it frequently myself—that the chief possession of a nation is its youth, and that is true. We are accustomed to repeat the Latin tag that "the greatest reverence is owed to youth." And that also is true. We must be most careful in the handling of youth, scrupulous to avoid discouragement and mis-direction. But in this handling we must show commonsense. You remember the story of the Scots girl who complained of her lover that he was "senselessly ceevil." We must not overdo our respectfulness. Youth has immense merits, but it has also great defects. It is eager, bold, adventurous, but it is also ignorant, inexperienced, unbalanced—it must be, or it would not be youth.

Now there is a foolish creed in some quarters to-day which says that children must never be checked or reprimanded, or in any way repressed; a creed based on

¹*Boy Scouts' Association Dinner. Toronto. 5th February, 1938.*

141

a false and trashy psychology. Every human being has to be checked and repressed, and if they do not get used to it in youth they will have to endure it in later life, when they are far less able to bear it. There should be nothing namby-pamby about our attitude to the young entry. We should treat it with affection and sympathy, but also with candour and with humour. "We are none of us infallible, not even the youngest of us," was the saying of a famous Cambridge don. I remember in a witty play in my young days that one of the characters declared that "the old-fashioned respect for youth was fast dying out." Well, I hope the wrong kind of mealy-mouthed respectfulness will die out. We should treat our young as healthy vigorous plants, and not as exotics in a conservatory, giving them all honest encouragement, but not being afraid, when they are silly, to tell them so. This discipline, this friendly frankness is what every wholesome young man needs, and desires.

That, gentlemen, is the line which the Scout movement has always taken, and it is a most valuable corrective to the faddists who would have children grow up untrained and uncorrected. We give our Scouts the ritual of a service, and without something of the kind no human being can be happy. We give them companionship, which rubs off their corners, we give them a fine code of conduct, and we offer a free development to every healthy youthful instinct. We keep them in close touch with nature, which is the greatest of all educators. We prepare them to be, in the fullest sense of the word, men and citizens.

The second reflection I would offer you to-night is this. Let the older men here cast their minds back thirty years, before the Scout movement had properly

started. Suppose that then you had been told that in
thirty years the Scout movement would have spread
over the whole earth and have a membership of hundreds of thousands of every race and nation. Suppose
you had been told that in its ranks there would be no
distinctions of class or religion, that its creed would be
based upon profound moral truths, that its fundamental
principles would be peace among men and the service
of our fellows. Suppose you had been told that great
international gatherings would be held periodically,
where Scouts from all over the world would meet and
fraternise. What would you have said? I think you
would have said that, if such a miracle came about,
then our civilisation would be secure and there would
be no more strife among men.

Yet the miracle has happened. But other things have
happened also. In these thirty years we have seen the
greatest and cruellest war known to history. To-day
we find the Scout movement flourishing, but we also
find the nations at loggerheads and peace very far off,
and the world near the edge of the abyss. What have
we to say about it? That the Scout movement, for all
its high purpose has failed, that its goodwill is a mere
drop in the bucket of the world's ill-will? No, gentlemen, I think not. I think that is a false deduction. I
think that those who thirty years ago made a hopeful
forecast were nearer the truth. I believe profoundly
that no great and honest effort of mankind can fail in
the long run. The leaven may be slow to work, but it
does work, and steadily leavens the whole. I believe
that the clouds which darken our sky to-day will pass,
and that when the sun shines again we shall discover
that we have builded better than we knew. The
optimists are wiser prophets than the pessimists.

BOY SCOUTS

4[1]

TO-NIGHT I have an audience which is largely
composed of Scout-masters and Rover-leaders and
Patrol-leaders and Cub-leaders, young men who are
actively engaged in the training and guidance of youth.
Now to be a leader you must have a purpose and a
policy; before you can guide others you must be able
to guide yourself. So I am going to suggest to you, in
all humility, as a much older man, one or two rules of
life. They will not be the ordinary copybook maxims.
Copybook maxims are, I think, the invention of middle-
aged people who are a little tired and discouraged by
the world, and they have not much attraction for youth.
They inculcate a drab, timorous and unimaginative
attitude to life which is the very last thing that young
men should believe in. But all the same some rules we
must have, for the world to-day is pretty difficult for
everybody. It is an age of confusion and disillusion,
and we need more than ever some kind of compass to
direct our steps.

The first rule of life, I would suggest to you, is that
you must be prepared to take risks. There is no more
hopeless motto for youth than "Safety first". I do not
mean that people should be foolhardy, that they should
choose, for preference, a profession in which they stand
a good chance of breaking their necks. But I mean that
they must be prepared for an honourable gamble in life.
They must play the long game and not the short game.

[1]*Boy Scouts' Association Dinner. Montreal. 18th February, 1939.*

Everybody has two careers open to him; one which is, so to speak, ready-made for him, and the other which he must make for himself. To slip into the first job which offers when you have no special aptitude for it and no interest in it; to think only of finding a niche, and not to make certain that it is the right niche—that is a certain road to disillusion and failure. Find out what there is to do and what you want to do, and insist on doing it, whatever the obstacles are and whatever the dangers.

My second piece of advice is about your brains. In most addresses to young men which I have come across there has been a great deal said about character, and too little, I think, about intelligence. But the one is just as important as the other; in fact I doubt if you can separate them. The British people, and I think the Canadian people also, are always a little inclined to over-estimate character because they pride themselves on the possession of it. The ordinary British attitude is something like this: "We do not profess to be more clever than our neighbours—perhaps we are not so clever—but we have more character, and that means that when we get into difficulties we always muddle through." I do not believe it. Nobody ever muddled through anything. In the Great War we muddled at the start and stuck fast in the mud; we won in the end because we had learned to use our brains better than our opponents. I want you to realise the extreme importance of making yourself really competent in whatever job you undertake. We live in a world to-day in which most of the problems are new problems, and in which intelligence is more needed than ever. These problems will never be solved by unstable, clever people with quick brains and nothing else. But neither will they be solved by honest stupidity. Character is the most important thing, no doubt, in life, but it must be illumined and directed by intelligence. If you have both you will not only be a successful man, but you will be a good citizen, the kind of citizen who will yet carry us through our troubles and help to create a better world.

Lastly, you must have some kind of creed and faith and purpose. I do not want you to take anything at second-hand, or believe in a thing because your father believed in it, or your schoolmasters believe in it. I think to-day there is a wholesome instinct abroad for construction, a wholesome revolt against chaos and confusion; but if you are to be constructive you must also be critical. We have to examine all the articles of our faith and discard those which are useless. But some faith we must have; something to which in the last resort we can hold fast at any cost. And it must be a positive faith, a passionate, determined belief that will carry us through the darkest days. Life is a very pleasant thing and a very amusing thing, but it is no good pretending that it is easy. If you are going to make anything of it you will have battles to fight; you will often be sick at heart, and you will need all the comfort and support you can get. There are many isms to-day to perplex us—Naziism, Communism, Fascism, and so forth—and a great nuisance they are! But most of them will cancel each other out. There is only one ism which kills the soul, and that is pessimism.

Now with any purpose in life there must be two main duties. The first is to preserve what is worth preserving, and the other is to hand on something new to your successors. I was once the Warden of an ancient Border castle which stands in a narrow pass, through which flows the river Tweed. I have often thought that that old keep typified some of the greatest duties of human life. In the first place it defended the pass and the neighbourhood; in the second place, in the old days of English invasion the beacon on the roof passed on the warning light from the Border to the capital city. These two duties are before every man, and they were never more vital in the world than to-day. We have to hold the pass, for many precious things are in danger. We have to hold the pass and defend our liberties and our heritage of civilisation. But we have also to hand on the light. We have received from our forefathers a mighty bequest. We must hand that on to our successors not only undiminished, but increased, for the only way in which we can pay our debt to the past is by putting the future in debt to ourselves.

BOY SCOUTS

5[1]

THIS is the fifth occasion on which I have had the privilege of being present at this annual dinner, and of meeting my friends who are interested in scouting. I can honestly say that nothing in my five years' tenure of office as Governor-General has given me more pleasure than my connection with the movement. It has brought me into touch with many men—busy men who are giving time and thought to the work—a most unselfish and worthy form of public service for there is no advertisement in it. Up and down the Dominion, too, wherever I have gone—and I have gone pretty far afield—I have found companies of Scouts inspired by the true Scout tradition, as fine specimens of youth as you will find in the world. I have learned from you a very great deal. You have given me far more than I have been able to give you. In leaving Canada not the least of my regrets is that I am parting from such a splendid company.

I think we may congratulate ourselves on a very real success. We have attained and passed the hundred thousand mark which we set as our goal. That in itself is a real achievement. But we have excelled not only in quantity but in quality. Their Majesties were profoundly impressed by what they saw of our Cubs and Scouts in their journey through the Dominion, and I can tell you that as Chief Scout I was proud of your achievement. But, gentlemen, we are not going to stop

[1]*Boy Scouts' Association Dinner. Toronto. February, 1940. (Read).*

148

there. There are over a million boys in Canada who might share in our movement, and as yet we have only got a tenth of them. So there is still ample room for expansion. As this is my last chance of addressing you I am going to venture to offer you a few suggestions as to the lines on which our future work should develop.

In looking at our figures I have been struck with the fact that our progress is in an inverse proportion to the age of our members. We have done wonderfully well with our Cubs; we have done very well with our Scouts, but we have a very small number of Rovers. It looks, therefore, as if our appeal was weakening as adolescence proceeds. Now I want to see this remedied. I want to see our movement made attractive not only to the boy but to the young man. Here in Canada, in this wonderful country which has still a frontier, there must be ways of catching the imagination and enlisting the interest not only of boyhood but of youth. Would it be possible, I wonder, to organise more fully expeditions not merely to summer camps, but right into the wilds, expeditions which would have a real flavour of exploration and adventure? Would it be possible, I wonder, to do what I understand has been done elsewhere, and bring scouting into touch with our development in the air? I believe that in these directions much might be done to attract adolescence.

I dwell especially upon the air, for one result of this war will be that Canada, with her tremendous air effort, will be in the very forefront of air development. When peace comes we shall have a very large body of trained airmen. That may be at first an awkward baby to hold; but, if I may be allowed to mix my metaphors, I do not think it will be impossible to liquidate that baby and to turn this war effort into a great asset of peace. I am, as you know, an enthusiast about the Canadian North, and the key to our northern development is in the air. I want to see our Scout movement keep this in mind. I want to see our Scouts add air-mindedness to their other qualities and attainments.

I would go further and venture to suggest to you that it is our business to link up our Scout training more closely with the practical problems which are facing our growing youth. We are giving our Scouts an admirable moral and physical discipline which is the true basis for a worthy and successful life. You cannot put the value of that too high. The problems of youth are more difficult today than ever before, and they are not going to be easier when this war is over. Cannot we, while these boys are in our charge, do more by advice and training to see that when they enter the grown-up world they will have a reasonable chance? Cannot we, while keeping in the forefront our moral and spiritual ideals, take pains to see that our Scouts, when they enter adult life, shall have a real chance to reap the fruit of their training, and shall not get into the wrong grooves, or into blind alleys which lead to a dead wall?

VII

A WORKING PHILOSOPHY

The Fortress of the Personality[1]

I HAVE been honoured to-day by a great University, which is the centre of light and learning in a great city. It would be an impertinence for me to attempt to praise you. Your achievements in science and scholarship have long since made you a familiar name in the world. But your most recent graduate may be permitted to offer you his heartfelt thanks for the honour you have paid him, his congratulations on the great things you have done in the past, and his hope, nay his certainty, of the brilliant career which still awaits you.

It is my duty, I understand, to say a few words to you this afternoon. I am glad to have the privilege, for I am always happy to have the chance of speaking to young men. All my life I have been connected with Universities, and, indeed, until the other day, I represented my own Scottish Universities in the British Parliament. But it is not easy for me to find a topic. Politics, of some kind or other, have hitherto been my chief subject; but politics now, I am glad to say—at least politics in the ordinary sense—are forbidden me. But to-day, when the duties and rights of the State impinge so much upon the private life of the citizen, politics, in the broadest sense, have become of far more universal interest than ever before. We realise that no nation can live for itself alone. We recognise that all of us are members of a community, whether it be city or nation, and that the individual's life can never again be

[1] *University of Toronto. Toronto. 27th November, 1935.*

153

an *enclave* secluded from his fellows. The public interest has become, in some sense, also every man's private interest. So I hope that I may be permitted to speak to you for a few minutes upon a topic which is partly political, but which is also most germane to a University, and to the future of you young men whom I see before me.

My old friend, James Bryce, when he was British Ambassador at Washington, spoke thus of the Universities in the United States. "Whereas" he said, "the Universities of Germany are popular, but are not free, and those of England are free, but not popular, yours, like those of Scotland, are both popular and free." Popular and free!—that is a great conception, and it is a conception which I think the University of Toronto has striven to live up to. The two words do not mean the same thing. An institution may be popular without freedom, and free without being popular. The combination, if it is achieved, means the attainment of the true democratic ideal, as I understand it—equality of social status, a high level of human sympathy, and complete freedom of thought.

We are told, and told truly, that to-day democracy is at stake. I do not quite know how to define the word. Lord Acton once counted over two hundred definitions of "liberty", and I think it would be possible for a laborious scholar to get as many definitions of "democracy". Primarily, of course, it is a particular mechanism of government. Now, no system of government has any sacrosanctity in itself; its value depends entirely upon how it is worked, and upon whether the conditions are suitable. The democratic form of government is the most difficult of all, because it sets before itself so high a purpose. It offers a wonderful prospect, and if it fails the disillusion is the keener. You remember that Herodotus lyrically talks about democracy as being a thing which is beautiful even in its name. And yet the generation after him was utterly disillusioned, and you find a Greek statesman dismissing it contemptuously as an "acknowledged absurdity". The true democratic ideal has never been attained in history. Human society has never yet risen to the perfect balance of law and liberty, and to-day the conditions of its attainment are more difficult than ever before.

But I am not going to talk to you about the political side. The democratic ideal has a far wider application than the mere technique of government. I can imagine a country with full representative institutions, with all the apparatus of freedom, where, nevertheless, the citizens lived in a spiritual bondage. And history has many examples to show of men dwelling under the harshest tyranny, who have yet preserved their freedom of soul. Popular forms of government have no value unless they foster in each individual the power of being himself, of standing squarely on his feet, and of living his life according to a law which is self-imposed, because it is willingly accepted. Let us consider for a minute or two the meaning of this spiritual democracy, without which no constitution, however liberal in form, is more than a tyranny and a bondage.

It means, if I may risk a definition, the safeguarding of the personality. Coming from England a month ago, we had a rather stormy and comfortless voyage, and I was reduced to the reading of St. Augustine. One phrase of that great man stuck in my memory, where he talks about "the abysmal depths of personality"— *abyssus humanae conscientiae.* It is the human soul which to-day is in danger; its integrity and independence. Our fathers devised a certain constitutional machine which they believed would safeguard this independence, and at the same time permit the tasks of government to be adequately performed. That machine may have been too narrowly constructed; in the interests of efficiency it may have to be drastically remodelled, for, as I have said, there is no plenary virtue in any one device. But what we must hold fast to is the truth that no machine can be permitted to impair the freedom of the spirit and weaken the citizen's responsibility towards that conscience and that reason which are the gifts of God.

The danger, as I see it, comes from two sources. One I should call the peril of Mass. In our modern state, with its vast aggregations of human beings, we are apt to think too abstractly. Phrases like "the workers", "the proletariat", "the bourgeoisie", "the intellectuals", obscure reason. Instead of a number of living, breathing, enjoying, suffering individuals, we think only of broad classes, and generalise about them with a fatal facility. It is due partly to a false scientific standpoint, which likes to deal with human nature in the lump. It is a dangerous tendency, for the result is that the State is apt to be thought of as an end in itself, and not as something which exists for the betterment of each citizen. The human being is obscured by the inhuman mass. I am no believer in a narrow individualism. The state, the organized community, is a thing of immense value—it is indeed the basis of civilisation; and there are a thousand directions in which communal powers may be rightly used, since they have a weight behind them denied to sporadic individual effort. But these powers are of value only in so far as they safeguard and fulfil the life of the citizen, and give to him or her a richer, more responsible, and, therefore, a freer life.

The second danger is what I would call the peril of the Machine. This tends not merely to blur the individuality of the human masses, but to leave out humanity altogether, and to regard the citizen as a minute cog in a vast impersonal mechanism. Efficiency is the watchword. The individual is squeezed and planed into a lifeless automaton. But efficiency has no meaning for the State, except in so far as it fosters human values. Otherwise we have a sterile conception of society where human values disappear altogether.

These dangers are incident to the advance of what we are accustomed to call civilisation. They are attended, no doubt, by an enormous increase in the material apparatus of life; but at the same time they nullify all that makes life worth living, and in the long run they must mean the disintegration of society. For, just as you cannot have a healthy league of nations without healthy nations, so you cannot have a wholesome society unless the units in it have a wholesome mode of life. The dangers are increased by something with which we have become too familiar in recent years throughout the world, and which is best described, I think, as a failure of nerve. There is panic abroad, and people run to any shelter from the storm. Certain great countries in the Old World have been prepared to surrender their souls to a dictator or an oligarchy, if only they are promised security. In such cases, all freedom of personality is lost, and human beings become a disciplined collection of automata.

Let us be very clear what freedom means. A free man is not one who is permitted to do as he likes; he is one who willingly accepts a discipline and makes it his own, because he understands its value. He is one who is clothed in loyalties, loyalties to family and race and birthplace, to parish, and province, and nation, and who is endowed with a multitude of cherished traditions. In a word, he is one who is permitted to develop that free complex of tastes, interests and ideas which we call personality. Only thus can he be a citizen in the true sense. Only thus can he be, in the full sense, a moral being; only thus can art and thought have any meaning for him. This truth has been well put by William Blake in some of his uncouth verses:

> "Art and Science cannot exist but in minutely organised
> Particulars,
> And not in the generalising Demonstration of the
> Rational Power.
> The Infinite resides alone in Definite and Determinate
> Identity."

Remember these are the words, not of a politician or of a sociologist, but of a poet and a prophet.

This blurring and crushing of personality, I would remind you, is an old evil in the world. Whenever a mechanical State has been contrived, the experiment has been attempted, and it has always ended in disaster. The Emperor Augustus was almost the only dictator in history who kept his head. He devised for the Roman Empire a stiff bureaucracy, a very marvellous instrument of government. But, being a wise man, he realised that this splendid machine would fail unless the individuality of the citizen were preserved, and he made every effort to put personality into Roman life by reviving old customs and by encouraging every kind of local idiom. He might have succeeded had his successors been of his own calibre; but they were not, and the experiment failed. Within a century or two the

Roman polity had become a mechanical thing, immensely efficient, giving, on the whole, peace and a reasonable prosperity to great masses of men, but fatally stunting and sterilizing the personality of the citizen. Deliverance came from the Christian faith, which, as part of its gospel, taught the freedom of the individual, and the transcendent worth of every soul in the sight of God.

I am speaking to members of a University, most of whom are at the beginning of their careers. If the main function of a University is, as I believe it to be, the guardianship of the central culture of mankind, the trusteeship of humane learning, then the preservation of this spiritual democracy must be a vital part of its purpose. Let me recur to James Bryce's words, "popular" and "free". We do not believe, like Rousseau, in any natural equality, for that is not how men are made. The old egalitarianism had never any foundation in fact, for men, in powers of mind and character, are created wildly unequal. But while spiritual democracy accepts natural gradations, it can have nothing to do with vulgar, artificial ones. It abhors social snobbery, and in practice it takes the sting out of the natural disparity between human beings by that strong human sympathy which is the only true leveller. Do you remember a passage in one of Rupert Brooke's letters, where he wrote: "I can watch a dirty, middle-aged tradesman in a railway carriage for hours, and love every greasy, sulky wrinkle in his weak chin, and every button on his spotty, unclean waistcoat." It has that kindly affection for every cranny of human nature which Sir Walter Scott, for example, had—a charity which finds nothing common or unclean, a power of looking at life with such clear and compassionate eyes that it can find in its ironies both mirth and pity—the quality which, I think, is best described by that noble word, "loving-kindness".

That is one side of this democracy. The other side is that it stands for complete freedom of thought, for the liberty of disinterested speculation. It will not tolerate any mass coercion upon the mind. The most august authority will not be allowed to dictate to it its thoughts and dreams. Its watchword is Plato's—"Life without the spirit of inquiry is not worth having"—*bios anexetastas ou biōtos*. And in the last resort its manifesto is Thomas Jefferson's famous words: "I have sworn upon the altar of God eternal hostility against every form of tyranny over the mind of man." For it knows that, though constitutions may crack and crowns may tumble down, though economic dogmas become fantastic and the foundations of the world seem to be crumbling, yet, so long as the sacredness of man's personality is preserved, civilisation is secure. This freedom of spirit is what you young men must most strictly preserve. Do not take your creed second-hand from anyone, but shape it for yourselves. You will make plenty of mistakes, but it is only by fresh and candid thought that you will work out a faith worth having. I would far rather have a young man talk the uttermost nonsense, provided it is his own, than repeat like a gramophone the sagacities of other people. He may be foolish, but it is better to be foolish than to be dead.

Has it ever struck you what a depth of meaning there is in the old phrase about "selling your soul?" We use it idly and loosely, as a metaphor without much meaning, but in earlier days, among simple folk, it meant the whole world. In the Middle Ages in a thousand stories, from the great tale of Faust down to the humblest folk lore of the North, you will find men and women confronted with the choice of pleasure and prosperity and ease upon the one side, and on the other the preservation of their integrity of spirit. The choice was regarded as momentous, a matter of life and death. And so it was. And so it still is. The personality must remain a virgin fortress, of which even the remotest out-works are jealously guarded. Man must continue to be the captain of his soul.

The Folly of the Wise[1]

I AM very glad to meet you all again, for I have the most happy recollections of the last time I addressed you, eleven years ago. So far as I remember, I talked to you then about British politics. Well, that subject is closed to me now, and so is every other kind of politics. But it is an excellent habit with your Canadian Clubs to permit your guests a very wide freedom of choice. So to-day I am not going to deliver you a solemn address. Let us rather consider it a conversation round a luncheon table, in which I egotistically choose the topic and monopolise the talk.

In this troubled time for the world at large, when people naturally strain their eyes into the mist to see if they can hope for better weather ahead, there is a great chance for the prophet. We all of us tend to prophesy about the future, and whether we are optimists or pessimists depends upon our temperament. I want to say a few words to you about the limitations of the prophet's business. Prophets are generally clever people, and I might call my topic the stupidity of the clever, the folly of the wise. It is a remarkable fact, which you will find all through history, that the very clever people, when they forecast the future, are nearly always wrong. It is the plain man who is far more often right.

Let me give you a few illustrations. Just before the French Revolution there were in Paris some very acute American observers, who, being detached from local

[1]*Canadian Club. Montreal. November, 1935.*

162

interests, might have been expected to take a balanced view of the situation, and to foresee the troubles ahead. But they did nothing of the kind. I found the other day a forecast by one of the best of them. He considered France a wonderfully settled State—a loyal people, under a popular King. But when he looked across the Channel at Britain he foresaw trouble there. He thought that at any moment there might be a popular uprising, and the end of the old regime. Yet what actually happened was that in two years came the fall of the Bastille and the beginning of the French Revolution, while in the twenty years that followed, Britain advanced not only to a premier place among world Powers, but to the beginning of liberalism and reform.

A little later we come to the Victorian era in Britain, the industrial revolution, a great advance in applied science, and an enormous increase in national prosperity. I fancy that the world has never seen a more secure and untroubled regime on the whole than that of the second half of the nineteenth century in England. There have never been people more secure in their faith and more confident about the future. But, looking back, it is curious how blind they were in their forecast of that future. Statesmen like Bright and Cobden, Palmerston and Gladstone, believed that the British form of constitutional democracy was not only certain to continue in Britain, but was destined to be the model which the whole world would adopt. Great scientists were convinced that they had found the key of the universe and that their creed was the last word in human wisdom. They could not conceive that any thinking man would ever question their dogmas. Yet what has happened? Our English constitutional liberalism, which at first was imitated by a considerable part of the globe, has now been almost everywhere rejected. As for the proud Victorian science, it has no doubt had enormous triumphs on the practical side, but to-day its fundamentals are being very widely questioned by the scientists themselves.

Here is another instance of judicial blindness. Matthew Arnold was in France in 1859, and he talked a good deal to Lord Cowley, the English Ambassador. They both agreed that the strength of France, from the military point of view, was unassailable. Lord Cowley gave it as his opinion that, supposing the whole German nation under arms came against her, she could easily ward them off with her left hand. Yet that was only eleven years before Sedan. [*]

Coming nearer our own times, let me give you the case of Lord Morley. He was a great scholar and a man of acute and masterful mind. He was also a most serious student of politics. But a few years before the World War began he wrote an essay in which he criticised Sir John Seely's dream of a united Empire. He took, as the *reductio ad absurdum* of that conception, the notion that it would ever be possible for Australia to contribute a penny to the expenses of a war fought to defend that neutrality of Belgium to which Britain was pledged. Yet a few years later Australia was not only contributing to the costs of the defence of Belgium, but her sons were fighting desperately on the continent of Europe for that very cause. Those of you who have read Mr. Duff Cooper's recent volumes on Lord Haig will remember another instance of the blindness of this eminent statesman. When Lord Morley was Secretary of State for India, Douglas Haig was Chief of Staff in India, and with Lord Minto's assent he prepared a

scheme for the use of the Indian Army abroad in case
Britain should be involved in a world war. Well,
Morley heard of it and promptly ordered that any such
kind of study should cease at once. He declared it
dangerous and nonsensical. He declared that it was a
waste of time even to raise such a question, since it was
manifestly beyond the sphere of the possible. Happily,
Douglas Haig disobeyed orders and did not scrap the
plan, and a decade later that plan was put into effect,
when Indian troops crossed the seas to fight in the
Great War.

Let me give you a personal reminiscence. Early in
1915, when I was at St. Omer at General Headquarters,
I used to ride every morning with Sir Henry Wilson.
Sir Henry's was one of the most acute and fertile minds
I have ever known, and every morning as we rode he
prophesied to me what was going to happen. I wrote
all these prophesies down in a little book, and in 1917
I confronted Sir Henry with them. Every one of them
had proved wildly wrong. I asked him for an explana-
tion. "Oh," he said, "my dear fellow, the trouble is I
am too clever."

One last illustration. In the year 1928 a celebrated
professor of economics at Harvard, whose name I will
mercifully withhold, wrote these words of the United
States; "There is absolutely no reason why the widely
diffused prosperity which we are now witnessing should
not permanently increase." These are the words of a
man who spoke with authority, but next year came the
great depression and—well, you know the rest of the
story.

What is the reason, I wonder, why these very clever
people have been so consistently blind? The only ex-
planation I can give is a simple one, what Senancour

called *le vulgaire des sages*, the folly of the wise. They are too clever, like Sir Henry Wilson. They over-intellectualise the world. They are too logical; they make history a simple pattern of cause and effect, which is not the truth. They do not allow for the unforeseen accident. More, they have no *flair* for the imponderable things which cannot be put into a straightforward argument. They work wholly by intellect, and are lacking in instinct.

This is just where the plain man scores. He is not intellectual. He is not too logical; but he has a curiously sound instinct, just because he is so close to real life, about what is actually going to happen. I will give you a famous example. George III could not be called a clever man. He was the plainest of plain men, much more of a farmer than a statesman, and it has been the custom, perhaps, to exaggerate his stupidity. But when the American Colonies were finally lost, and someone commiserated with him on the subject, he replied that he did not think he really minded; for, said he, "America is going to have awful troubles of her own. Mark my words. Within the next century there is going to be a desperate conflict between North and South." So you see, this plain, stupid fellow forecast the great American Civil War eighty years before it happened. I remember at the beginning of the Great War, when everyone talked about a short war, a certain regimental officer coming to see me—he was ultimately killed as a Brigadier at Passchendaele—and prophesying. He said, "The war will last for four years, and it will be won at the end chiefly by the British Empire." I said I supposed by the British navy. He said, "No, by the British army, which, at the end of the war, will be the strongest in the world." I thought he was talking nonsense, but he was right.

Let me give you an imaginary case. Suppose a clever man in the spring of 1914 had been presented with a vision in which he was assured of certain facts twenty years ahead. He was assured of the facts, but not of their effect. He knew that Britain's National Debt would increase from 700 millions to 8,000 millions; that the cost of her social services would rise from 24 millions to 220 millions; that her foreign trade, which was regarded as the basis of British industry, would suffer an enormous decline—coal from 73 million tons to 39 million; the value of cotton piece goods from 122 million to 58 million pounds; certain iron and steel products from 37 million to 16 million; ships for export from 11 million to two and a half million. What would have been his conclusion? Without doubt that Britain would be finally and irretrievably bankrupted and ruined, and he would have had unanswerable arguments to support his view. But what are the facts? The credit of Britain to-day stands higher than ever; the standard of living is far higher than it was in 1914; the vital statistics indicate a greatly improved standard of health; there has been a remarkable growth in the savings and investments of the poorer classes. The prophecy of our wise man, based upon a knowledge of certain facts, but not of their consequences, would have been monstrously beside the mark. Now, what would the plain man have said in 1914 if confronted with the same facts? No doubt he would have been horribly scared. But I do not think he would have believed that the consequences would be national disaster. His answer would have been very much the answer which Adam Smith, on his death-bed, gave to a pessimist who told him that the country was ruined. "Young man," he said, "there is a deal of ruin in the country." The ordinary man in 1914 would have believed that somehow or other we would worry through. And the ordinary man would have been right.

No, gentlemen, it is very clear that prophesying is a gratuitous form of error, as someone has said, or, as someone else has said, an erroneous form of gratuity. The trouble is that it is usually done by very clever people, for the ordinary man does not prophesy. The clever people have too much intellect and too little instinct. That is why they are not very popular. That is why in older days the prophet was very frequently stoned.

I have presented you with what has always seemed to me to be an historical conundrum. There is a moral to be drawn from it, and that is, that we should never distrust the instinct and judgment of the ordinary man, which he may be quite unable to defend by detailed argument. That is really the basis of democracy —the belief that the whole people, in any great question, are generally more nearly right than any aristocracy or a coterie. There is a story of Lord Mansfield, the great English judge, who appointed a certain country gentleman, who knew no law, to be Chief Justice on one of the West Indian islands. He gave him this advice. "Base your judgments," he said, "upon your own commonsense, and you will be practically always right; but, for heaven's sake, don't attempt to give any reasons for them, for, if you do, since you know no law, they will be certainly wrong." There are two eternal types of human mind. There is the man whose judgment is mostly wrong, but who can give unanswerable reasons for it. And there is the man who can give no reasons at all, but who is mostly right. The second is, I am glad to think, the predominant type among our countrymen.

The Double Life[1]

I AM glad to accept the invitation of your Editors to send a message for their Spring issue. You are to regard this, please, as strictly a message, which might have been delivered to the Graduates' Society by word of mouth if I had been able to get you together. In the Oxford colleges with which I am familiar, the Visitor, who is generally an eminent Prelate, seems to be so called because he never visits them. I do not mean to interpret my office in that sense, for I hope to visit you often. Meantime I have the privilege of talking to you for a minute or two.

I am not going to attempt a homily on the meaning of a university, but I should like to tell you quite simply one thing my university experience has meant to me.

My first university was Glasgow, a place in many ways very like McGill. I went there at sixteen, according to the old Scottish fashion. My three years there were a strenuous time. The session lasted from October to April, and every morning I had to walk four miles to the eight o'clock class through all the varieties of unspeakable weather with which Glasgow, in winter, fortifies her children. I remember mornings of fog and snow and drenching rain, and also wonderful winter sunrises, when the dingy Clyde became a river of enchantment. I was a most inconspicuous student, and I won prominence only at the Rectorial elections. One especially I remember, where, against my convictions, I chose to support the Liberal colours, because I had

[1] "The McGill News". Montreal. Spring, 1936.

169

heard of the Liberal candidate, Mr. Asquith, but not of his opponent. I nearly came by my end at the hands of a red-headed Conservative savage, who is now the ex-Cabinet Minister, Lord Horne.

A Scottish university was a wonderful education in true democracy. On the benches of the Humanity class I sat between one man who was the son of a Hebridean crofter and spent his summers earning his livelihood by fishing, while on my other side was an Ayrshire ploughman, who went back in the spring to the plough. One is now a famous minister of the Scottish Church and the other high in the Indian Civil Service. It was a wonderful education in another way, for we had great teachers. Gilbert Murray taught me Greek, and A. C. Bradley English literature, and Henry Jones the rudiments of philosophy. I began as a mathematician, presently turned to classics (in which I won an Oxford scholarship), and finished as an ardent philosopher. So at the age of eighteen I had acquired certain interests which have never left me. A love for literature I always possessed, deriving it from its only true source, a cultivated home.

A Scottish university in those days had one supreme advantage. The session only lasted for half the year. After a winter of hard work I became for six months an unlettered vagabond, wandering about Scotland on an old bicycle in the quest of trout. I am not sure that these long idle summers were not the best part of my education.

When I went to Oxford I entered a very different atmosphere, what Stevenson has called a "half-scenic life of gardens." At first I disliked the place intensely, but I ended by falling most deeply under its spell. It smoothed out the prig and the barbarian in me, and, I hope, gave me a reasonable perspective in life. There I added history to my other interests. In the study of philosophy it seemed to me far behind Glasgow, but, on the other hand, its curriculum meant a minute acquaintance with certain immortal books such as Plato's *Republic* and Aristotle's *Ethics*, a training which I still believe to be one of the best in the world.

I went up to Oxford determined that my life should be that of a scholar. But during my four years there my attitude changed. I discovered that I wanted to do something more active and practical, and decided to go to the Bar. It was not an easy choice, for strong efforts were made to induce me to stay on and teach philosophy, but I think I decided wisely, for I should never have been happy as a don.

Since then I have had many professions—lawyer, business man, soldier, Government official, politician. But my university life has given me a permanent background, the value of which I should like to suggest to you. I am not going to speak of the merits of a university education on the social and human side, or of its importance in vocational training. That you know all about. I would rather emphasize its value in enriching one's private life. It provides certain permanent intellectual interests which are always there in the background as a refuge and a refreshment. Up to the War my chief interest was in philosophy. Since the War it has been more in the direction of history. But I have always tried to have one or two subjects on hand on which I worked, and which engaged a different part of oneself from that which was employed in earning one's bread. You may call it a hobby, but it was a hobby taken quite seriously. I found it a great relief to be able to turn from day-to-day practical affairs to a

world in which there was no "turbid mixture of con-
temporaneousness," and where the only aim was the
pursuit of truth. The work was often laborious, but it
was a different kind of labour, and therefore a relaxation.

Interests such as I have suggested keep a man or a
woman young. I have known successful men who have
made a great reputation through the way in which they
employed their leisure. The late Lord Balfour was such
a case. He could always find relief from the confused
world of politics in the purer air of science and philosophy. So was the late Walter Leaf. Banking is an
arduous enough business, but Walter Leaf not only
made himself one of the leaders of British banking but
was perhaps our greatest authority on the Homeric
poems. I could give you many other examples. I
know a famous engineer who is also a most competent
philosopher; an eminent Civil Servant who has made
remarkable contributions to mathematical science; a
member of the British Cabinet who is a first-rate
ornithologist; a successful business man who has made
a profound study of Chaucer, and another who knows
everything there is to be known about Polar exploration.
You may make use of the results of those leisure em-
ployments and win fame, or you may keep them for
your own private delectation; but the point is that they
lift the mind out of its groove and give it a happy playground to which it can constantly turn for refreshment.
They preserve your vitality, and they keep old age at bay.

So my last word to you on the value of university
training is that it enables a man to lead a Double Life!
That sounds a shocking piece of advice for your Visitor
to give you. But if you think it over, I believe you
will agree that it is sound. And I hope you will forgive
the egotism of these remarks. After all, you invited it!

THE MODERATE MAN[1]

IT is my privilege to address you shortly to-day, and in looking about for a subject it seemed to me that, as I am speaking principally to those who are just entering upon their careers, I might say something about a type of character which I believe to be estimable and worthy of all imitation, but which for the moment is unfashionable. We are living in a confused and difficult world, and in such a time the human mind is pre-disposed to hasty conclusions. We are all inclined to look for some short cut out of our troubles, some violent course which will shift things suddenly into a new orbit. Patience, reasonableness, what we call commonsense, are apt to seem counsels of despair. The moderate man is at a discount. This morning I would venture to say a few words on his behalf.

Moderation in the ordinary sense is not supposed to have much attraction for youth. It is assumed to be an attribute of disillusioned middle life, or even of old age. Youth desires to take the Kingdom of Heaven by storm, and has little love for the half-hearted or even for the temperate. Its model is Hotspur, not Nestor. It is shy of prudential counsels and the maxims of commonsense. Its power lies in its enthusiasm. The familiar French proverb, *Si jeunesse savait, si vieillesse pouvait*—"If only youth had knowledge, if only old age had power"—points to a popular belief that certain endowments and functions are incompatible. Vitality cannot co-exist with wisdom; wisdom involves laggard

[1]*Queen's University. Kingston. 7th November, 1936.*

feet, weakened sinews and a faint heart. The moderate man is eternally ineffective.

I would suggest to you that this view is a fallacy, for it accepts a shallow definition of moderation. It assumes that it is the stark opposite of enthusiasm. But the man of energy need not be the "rash, inconsiderate, fiery voluntary". The wise man need not be a sort of Buddha who is content to sit still and twiddle his thumbs. Coleridge said that no great thing was ever accomplished without enthusiasm, and that is simple truth; works are impossible without faith. But I wish to divest the word moderate of the sinister associations which are apt to surround it, and offer the moderate man to you as a type most worthy of imitation, a type more valuable, more effective and, I think, more genuinely attractive than the mere fighting man, whose head is filled with battle-cries which he imperfectly understands.

The opposite of the moderate is not the enthusiast, but the fanatic. But before we can find a proper definition of him we must get out of the way that false moderation which often usurps the name. The false moderate is that dreary type of being who, when confronted with a problem, always tries to halve the difference. His notion is to keep in the centre of the road. But this mechanical, mathematical calculation is useless in the real world. Practical life is not a narrow ridge where a pedestrian naturally keeps as near the centre as possible. It is much more like a difficult estuary of a river, where there are shoals in the centre as well as at the sides. The false moderate keeps in the middle of the channel, and presently is on a sandbank. The true moderate, with a chart of the course, and using all the knowledge and wits God has given him, may steer one hour close to one bank, and the next hour close to the other. His business is not to keep in the mathematical centre, but to find deep water. On the moral side the fault of the false moderate is spiritual apathy. He does not care enough about any cause to be extreme. He is tolerant because he is careless.

Our moderate, therefore, must not owe his point of view to the fact that he believes that every controversy can be settled by halving the difference, or because he is so sluggish and timid that his permanent resting-place is naturally the fence. We shall understand him better if we look for a moment at his opposite, the fanatic.

We can find that character in his simplest form in the history of religion. Let us take examples as near as possible to our own day—in the paradox produced by the Reformation. I say the paradox, because the essence of the Reformation was the restoration of the importance of the individual soul and of the value of the individual judgment. Properly interpreted, this attitude should have made for toleration, and such, in fact, was the view taken by liberal theologians in the seventeenth century. In their view the Bible, and not an historic church, was the palladium of Christianity; but the Bible was subject to the ultimate tests of conscience and reason. "The authority of man," said Hooker, "is the key which openeth the door of entrance into the Scriptures."

But the first business of the Reformers was church-making—to set up a rival institution in place of historic Catholicism. If emphasis were laid upon the individual judgment there was a danger of anarchy. The Bible was the foundation, no doubt, and must be in the hands of every Christian, but a strict canon of interpretation must be established. So we find a really great man,

John Calvin, in his *Institutes* laying down an absolute canon of Scripture teaching, a doctrine outside of which there could be no salvation. The view of the liberal theologians, that since human reason was the ultimate guide to the interpretation of the Scriptures, diversity of opinion was inevitable and, indeed, essential, was condemned as the ultimate heresy. The right of private judgment was wholly denied. John Milton wrote, "If a man believe things only because his pastor says so, though his belief be true, yet the very truth he holds becomes his heresy." But this attitude was anathema to those who accepted the fanatical point of view, even to men of a far gentler and humaner temper than Milton.

I am not going to inveigle you into the deeps of theological speculation. You will find the fanatical temper in every church, in every creed, in every department of human thought and action. The rigid Calvinist of the old school who condemned mankind to eternal torments except for a handful of his own communion; the rigid anti-Calvinist who identified religion with the observance of certain physical rites; the revivalist with his emotional short-cut to heaven; the secularist to whom all spiritual religions are a form of insanity; the devotee of Mrs. Grundy and her conventions, and the equally narrow and conventional hater of conventions and preacher of moral anarchy; the political die-hard who will drop not one jot of a creed which he learned from his grandfather or his grandmother; the rootless progressive who is crazy about anything however foolish provided it is new—all these are victims of the virus of fanaticism.

You see what it involves. In the first place it means a surrender of the reason. A formula is accepted as the ultimate truth, and about this they will not argue. Their minds are atrophied and only a little bit of them works, but to that little bit they add all the weight of character and emotion. They believe profoundly in their crudities, and they accept the fact that their faith is emotionally strong as a guarantee that it is also intellectually sound. The basis of all fanaticism is a partial atrophy of the mind.

In the second place fanaticism involves an undue simplification of life. Every false doctrine, every fanaticism, depends upon a mechanical instead of an organic conception of the world. The revolutionary who believes that all antecedent history can be neglected, that the slate can be sponged clean, and that he can write upon it what he pleases, is as much a victim of the simplification fallacy as the Covenanting divine who believed that, when he excommunicated a man or a sect, his act was promptly ratified by the Recording Angel.

Let us make no mistake about fanaticism. It is a very powerful thing, and its power comes from its narrowness. It does not suffer from a divided mind. Again and again in human history there have come times when the immediate problem seemed simple, and when latitude of mind meant weakness of mind. There is only a certain quantity of spiritual force in any man, and if it is spread over too broad a surface the stream will become shallow and languid. Fanaticism has done great things in history, but these things have almost invariably been destructive—necessary destruction, perhaps, but still destruction. Moreover, there is always the certainty that it will induce a counter-fanaticism. An arbitrary conception of the Divine will induce an arbitrary denial of its existence at all. A fanatical glorification of the powers of the State will produce as its corrective a fanatical individualism. The fanatic may do valuable work in burning down a crazy structure, but the constructive work, the erection of a new home for mankind, is a task for the moderate. It is the Meek, in the most literal and practical sense, who inherit the earth.

We are now in a position to examine the meaning of true moderation.

In the first place it involves a certain critical standpoint, a certain degree of honest scepticism. The critically constructive mind, the constructively critical mind, is needed to-day in a special degree, and it should be found particularly among those who, like you, have access to the treasures of the world's literature and thought. We need intellectual courage, the courage to ask questions and insist upon an answer.

In the second place the moderate man must keep his mind bright and clear. He must reverence human reason, not because it is infallible, but because it is the best thing we have got. I am not going to embark upon the eternal philosophical discussion as to the relative value of reason and intuition. Both are necessary. I am the last man to deny the value of that instinct which cannot be expounded by any rational process. There are spheres where the ratiocinative powers of man cannot function, and where the bold leap of faith and imagination must take the place of plodding logic. We have no lack of witnesses to the value of those high moods of the soul. We have Euripides, for example—the great passage in the *Bacchae*—

> Knowledge, we are not foes;
> I seek thee diligently,
> But the world with a great wind blows,
> Shining, and not from thee.

We have Tertullian's famous *Credo quia impossibile*.
We have the saying of St. Ambrose which was Newman's favourite quotation: *Non in dialectica Deo com-
placuit salvum facere populum suum*—"Not by cold logic
does God purpose to save his people."

Yes, but the recognition of this fact does not justify a
revolt against the rational. For nine-tenths of life is
capable of analysis and judgment by the human reason,
and in such cases to refuse to reason its rights is a crime
against humanity. In some form or other the process
which Hegel has defined as thesis, antithesis and syn-
thesis must be gone through if we are to reach truth.
Intuitions which claim the sanctity of a religious faith
and decline the test of reason will almost inevitably
land us in trouble. They *may* transcend any rational
process, but we must make certain of that fact by first
of all submitting them to the test of reason.

The fanatic lives only on his instincts. Take a
countryman of mine who is deservedly held in high
esteem, John Knox. He did a great work, and he also
did an infinity of mischief, and the mischief was largely
due to the fact that he lived wholly by flaming intuitions. His mind was incapable of ordinary logic. If
you study his controversial work you will be amazed by
its crudity and confusion. His Catholic opponents had
almost invariably the better of the argument. Had
John Knox been able to marry to his intuitive powers a
respect for the human reason, and the gift of using it, the
history of seventeenth century Scotland would have been
very different. Remember, the man whose conclusions
are derived from a rational process respects those who
differ from him, for he understands their case, having himself examined it, while to the non-rational intuition-
ist the case of an opponent is merely a blind perversity.

In the third place the true moderate has moral courage. The false moderate, of course, has no courage at all. The fanatic has a certain degree of courage, but not the highest kind. You will hear people talking about taking a bold line, about sticking to their principles, about backing their side. But that noisy clamour is usually a sign not of strength but of weakness. Extreme courses are easy to follow. They only require blind eyes and a hot temper, and the kind of courage which temper gives. It is a far more courageous thing to insist upon facing the facts, even when they involve the surrender of part of your creed. One of my predecessors here, Lord Minto, when he was Viceroy of India, laid down in a public speech a principle which seems to me to deserve to rank as one of the great maxims of public conduct. "The strongest man," he said, "is the man who is not afraid to be called weak."

Have you ever considered what that passage in the Bible means: "They shall mount up with wings as eagles, they shall run and not be weary, they shall walk and not faint"? It sounds like an anti-climax, like a descent from the greater to the less. But I think that the meaning is exactly the opposite. It is an ascent from the easy to the difficult. It is the last feat which is the hardest. It is not so difficult in a great crisis to rise like eagles; it is not so difficult in moods of excitement to run and not be weary. But most of the world's work has to be done at a foot's pace, and the hardest task of all is to walk the prosaic roads of life and not faint.

Lastly, true moderation involves a certain intellectual modesty and a sensitive humanity. You cannot have humanity without humility. You cannot understand your neighbour's point of view if you are too dogmatic about your own, just as you cannot sympathize with your neighbour's troubles if you are too much occupied with your own. One feature of fanaticism is its over-weening pride. It does not try to understand its op-ponents. It is content to despise them. I cannot think that that is a fruitful attitude in public or in private life. I commend to you rather the maxim of the old Irish Bishop Malachi in the eleventh century, who thus summarized the stages of human progress, *Spernere mundum, spernere sese, spernere nullum*. You begin by despising the world, you go on to despise yourself, and you end by despising nothing and nobody.

May I offer you in conclusion a shining example of true moderation? It is Abraham Lincoln. You remem-ber the circumstances under which he became President of the United States. He was strongly opposed to slavery, but he had none of the narrow fanaticism on the subject which characterized the Abolitionists of the North. His business was to keep the nation united and to effect a great reform without disruption. You remember the famous letter in which he wrote: "I would save the Union. I would save it the shortest way under the Constitution. . . . If I could save the Union without freeing any slaves, I would do it; and if I could save it by freeing all the slaves, I would do it; and if I could save it by freeing some and leaving others alone, I would do that." When the Southern States broke away he had to face a desperate problem. He was a President elected by a minority vote. He had a thoroughly disloyal Cabinet, most of whose members sneered at him as a self-educated country lawyer. He was the most pacific of men, with a deep horror of war. He had no army to speak of, and all the best soldiers had cast in their lot with the South. Could he by any conceivable means coerce by victory in the field five

and a half million people back into the Union? He was
no fire-eater, but a cautious and diplomatic statesman.
You remember how he angled for the allegiance of the
border States and said that he hoped to have the
Almighty on his side, but he must have Kentucky.

Well, he had to think out his problem without any
help, and he decided for war. He resolved that he must
fight to prevent democracy making a fool of itself. To
most of his colleagues it seemed an absurdly narrow
ground, a mere debating issue; but to Lincoln it was an
issue of the first importance, and the world has decided
that he was right. Having made up his mind, the
moderate became the enthusiast. He never lost his
reasonableness, his gentleness and his wisdom, but he
strove inflexibly for victory. The fanatics were all
prepared, at various times, to throw up the sponge, but
Lincoln, the moderate, never thought of surrender. He
was determined to wage war, as he said, to the last cent
and the last drop of blood, for only by a complete and
final victory could he safeguard the Union. It was the
same with his great opponent in the South, General
Robert Lee. He, too, was a moderate, and only reached
his decision after exhausting every other method, and
after the most painful self-examination. But having
decided, he was inflexible. The ordinary fire-eaters of
the South might crack and waver, but Lee, the moderate, never faltered.

In Lincoln you have, to my mind, the greatest
modern example of true moderation—of the spiritual
power which comes not from a hot head and a hasty
mind, but from a sincere reasonableness, complete intellectual candour, and that humility which realizes
that human nature is at the best fallible, and which is
purged of all arrogance and pride. I commend him to

your study. The fires of moderation are slow to kindle, but once lit they do not go out until they have burned up much rubbish and opened a path for the advance of mankind to a better country.

The spirit which I have tried to define has never been more necessary in the world than to-day. It is a change of heart rather than a change of mechanism which is the crying need. The revulsion from the brutalities of war in 1918 was not strong enough to bring about that clear-eyed and single-hearted effort which alone could insure the peace of the world. There were still too many fevers in the nations, and these fevers have remained as acute irritants, inflaming the eyes and distorting the mind. It is the duty of honest and public-spirited men to endeavour patiently and resolutely to bring the world back to a saner mood and a wiser temper. And that is a task in which all can help. It is a task in which our British Commonwealth especially can help with its sober realism, its steadfast good sense, and its long tradition of internal peace.

There was a famous Church Father in the Middle Ages, Bernard of Clairvaux, who wrote a Latin hymn, some lines of which are always haunting my mind. "Who will achieve universal peace?" he asks, and his answer is: "The disciplined, the dedicated, the pure in heart and the gentle in spirit." Every lawyer knows that the wisest law will not succeed unless it is in tune with the spirit of a people. If it is too far ahead of that spirit it will be a dead letter. No machinery which the wit of man can frame for peace will work unless there is behind it in the world at large the proper temper of mind. To create and maintain that temper is the first duty of civilized men.

QUALITY AND QUANTITY[1]

I WOULD like to say a few words to you to-day on the importance of quality. But first let us be clear about our definitions. Mass, spacial extension, numbers—these are not things to be despised. What has been called the "quantitative basis of qualitative development" is a fact of which we must take respectful note. A unit may be too small in quantity to achieve perfection in quality, just as it may easily be too big. A sapling will never grow to be a forest tree in a flowerpot. A neat laboratory experiment may have very little value unless it can be extended to a larger use. But quantity is futile unless it be permeated and dominated by quality. The science of war provides us with an illustration. Napoleon said quite truly that Providence was on the side of the bigger battalions. Yes, battalions; not hordes. Wars are won by superior strength, by weight of numbers, if the numbers are properly trained and supplied. But mere hordes will achieve nothing. They must be disciplined and directed; that is to say, they must be interpenetrated by quality.

There is a danger that this truth may be forgotten to-day. In the last half-century we have enormously enlarged and perfected the mechanical apparatus of living. That means that not only have we made the conditions of life more comfortable and pleasant, that we have reduced friction and saved ourselves much monotonous toil. It means also that we have acquired

[1]*McMaster University. Hamilton. 4th November, 1937.*

a new power over inanimate things, a power of which we cannot foretell the limits. We can attain a speed of movement which a generation ago was unthinkable. We have the mastery of certain forms of physical force which can literally move mountains. We have telescoped the world so that distance means little, and the margin of the unknown is fast vanishing.

All this miraculous advance is a triumph of the human mind. Yes, but the mind having thus triumphed cannot leave its work uncompleted. The danger is that we find ourselves overweighted by our very triumphs over matter, and, instead of using them, are used and dominated by them. What is the advantage of our being able to move ourselves with unparalleled speed about the globe if we have no serious purpose in our journeys? What value is our new control over physical force unless, by means of it, we can better the life of man? By our inventions we have caused distances to shrink, but, unless we are careful, we shall have the nations going to war to get standing-room and breathing-space on a shrunken globe. We have created a gigantic machine, but, unless we can use it, it will make use of us to our detriment. Our task, our urgent task, is to adapt it to the higher purposes of humanity. I confess that I am afraid when I hear people gloating over the marvels of scientific development and forgetting the toil which lies before us in harnessing our creations to the uses of a better life. Whatever is not reduced to the scale of human values is a monster, and a monster is always to be feared. You remember the phrase in the *Odyssey* about the Queen of the Laestrygones? "She was as tall as a mountain *and they hated her*." The Greeks had a proper detestation of monsters.

A few months ago I had occasion to take part in a

broadcast by which messages from different Governors-General in the Empire were listened to by a London audience. As I heard these messages—from Calcutta and Ottawa and Melbourne and Wellington and Cape Town—as clearly as if they had been spoken by men in the same room, I had a fresh realisation of the miracle of wireless telephony. But I reflected that our amiable platitudes were scarcely worthy of such an august transmission, and I wondered if we were capable of rising to the height of our opportunities and providing a spiritual content adequate to this new mastery over the material. We can speak now with a living voice to the ends of the earth. But have we anything to say? I seemed to realise as never before what vain things mass and quantity were unless inspired by quality.

This is a very old moral that I am trying to point, for it is a moral which wise men have preached since the beginning of human society. It is the moral of the Bible, that it is small profit to gain the whole world if you lose your soul. The spirit is in eternal conflict with matter until it transforms it and subdues it to its own purposes. Then the strife ends and quantity becomes also quality, and Browning's words in "Rabbi Ben Ezra" come true—

> "Let us not always say
> 'Spite of this flesh today
> I strove, made head, gained ground upon the whole!'
> As the bird wings and sings,
> Let us cry, 'All good things
> Are ours, nor soul helps flesh more now
> than flesh helps soul.' "

Man's business is to master his environment; to be, as the phrase goes, on the top of his job. There is a beautiful passage at the close of Plato's *Phaedrus*, when Socrates and Phaedrus, after discussing many things,

turn homeward in the afternoon. But before they leave
the grove by the Ilissus Socrates observes that one
should not leave the haunt of Pan without a prayer.
And this is his prayer—"Oh auspicious Pan, and ye
other deities of this place, grant to me to become
beautiful inwardly, and that all my outward goods may
prosper my inner soul." That was 2,300 years ago. If
that prayer was needful in the old simple days of
Hellas, it is still more needful to-day.

Let us look at the matter from another angle. There
is no branch of human activity in which grandiosity is
more easy or more fatal than the business of government. History is strewn with the wreckage of great
systems which swelled in size till, like a pyramid set up
on its apex, they fell from sheer excess of weight. We
are agreed, I think, that in a commercial concern there
is a limit of magnitude enforced by the limits of human
capacity; too vast a business will get beyond the power
of man's efficient management. It is the same with
governments. The famous empires of the East grew up
like gourds and perished because their roots had no
depth of soil. The empire of Alexander the Great
scarcely survived its founder. The Roman Empire was
different. I have been for some years a student of the
work of Augustus, almost the only dictator in history
who kept his head, and I have been impressed by the
wisdom of his conceptions. He was no megalomaniac,
and he detested rhetoric. He created a huge bureaucracy, which was necessary for efficient administration,
but he laboured always to preserve local idioms and to
foster individuality in the citizens. He never tried to
coerce his empire into the bonds of a mechanical
formula, and he refused to enlarge its territories. The

result was that the Roman Empire, in the form he gave it, endured for nearly four centuries; in a modified form it lasted for fourteen; and many of its foundations continue to-day.

What of our own British Empire? I remember that when I was a very young man a new vision seemed to dawn upon our people of the magnitude of our heritage. The prophet was Cecil Rhodes, the practical statesmen were Chamberlain and Milner, and the poet was Rudyard Kipling. In that vision there were noble and wise elements which have not perished. But there was also a heady strain which was its weakness, and which made people exult in the vulgarity of mere magnitude. That was before the day of coloured shirts in politics, but it was the day of coloured maps, and we were too fond of gloating over the red patches on the atlas of the globe. We were inclined to grandiloquence and rhetoric in our perorations at imperial banquets. We were prone to boast of having an Empire on which the sun never set— but, as Mr. Chesterton once said, there is not much charm in an Empire which has no sunsets! In a word, we were in peril of worshipping quantity and size and mass.

I think that that danger has gone. The rise of Dominion nationalism meant an attempt to give a specific idiom and quality to what had been formerly little more than geographical expressions. The tragedy of the Great War did much to banish boastfulness from our minds. We acquired a new humility, and with humility wisdom. To us in the British Commonwealth to-day mere size has no value in itself; it is only an added responsibility. We realise that quantity is a debit, not an asset, unless it can be translated into quality.

But, while the problem is recognised, it is not solved. It remains the ultimate problem before the British Commonwealth, before Canada, before the United States, and because it is a problem shared by them all, it is a strong bond of union between the English-speaking peoples. All three have acquired great possessions, which, according to how they use them, may be a curse or a blessing. Britain, with her Indian and Colonial empire, controls some of the richest producing grounds in the world, and is responsible for the well-being of many million people of different races and traditions. Her task is to use the discoveries of science in order to get from her vast estate the maximum value, for the world's production is as yet far from adequate to the world's capacity of consumption; and to assist the varied peoples in their advance towards civilisation and self-rule. If she were to use her great assets only for her selfish interests and forget her duty of trusteeship, then her power would be as short-lived as the over-grown empire of sixteenth-century Spain. The United States has to integrate her vast population, drawn from many stocks, into an organic unity, with, as a common denominator, a single political faith; and she has to adjust all her great resources so that they are not foolishly squandered or selfishly exploited. Canada has the task of developing assets as great as those possessed by any nation, for the use of herself and of the world. She has to make her wide spaces a land of homes; she has to push the frontier of knowledge and development still further north, and turn to human uses what till the other day was a no-man's-land; she has to join in a common patriotism citizens of many races; she has to annihilate the distances which separate by means of the purpose which unites. For each, for

Britain and the United States and Canada, the problem is the same. Quantity has to be transformed into quality, and mass and space brought under the dominion of the human spirit.

Will you permit me, gentlemen, to apply my moral to a matter which touches all of us? We pride ourselves on being a democracy, in which Everyman has in the last resort some share in the government. Public opinion, when it is awakened, must rule; and we believe that disciplined and informed public opinion is both the wisest and the safest ruler. It is a faith which is threatened to-day on many sides by other creeds, which differ widely among themselves, but which to my mind have this common characteristic, that they think of the State as a machine, of men and women as a mass, and crush and blur that most precious thing, the individuality of the citizen. Now, if democracy is to be preserved, its supporters must not fall into the same error. We have been too apt in the past, even we democrats, to think in terms of mass. We have been apt merely to count heads and to regard a majority as something sacred in itself. But to govern by majority is only a convenient method; it has no merit unless we make certain that that majority is instructed and has a reasonable chance of being right.

Democracy, in my view, is the best method of government which the human mind has yet devised; but it is also the most difficult. A dictatorship, an oligarchy, are far easier systems to work. Democracy demands a high level of education and intelligence and individual freedom, of discipline and public spirit. It can endure only if quantity is transformed into quality. So I conclude with a paradox which I believe to be true, that

democracy will only succeed if it becomes an aristocracy, in the classical sense of the word, where the rule of
the Many is also the rule of the Best. I am speaking to
young men and women on the threshold of life, and I
offer you this maxim. It is the duty of all of you to be
aristocrats. Of the aristocrat I know only one adequate
definition. He is the man who gives to the world more
than he takes from it.

VIII

THE LEARNED PROFESSIONS

ENGINEERING[1]

I AM here to-night to congratulate the Engineering
Institute of Canada on fifty years of vigorous and
fruitful life. Some time ago you honoured me by
making me an honorary member of the Institute, a
distinction of which I am very proud, for I have no
knowledge of engineering to justify it. I have had a
good many different professions in my life, and at
various times I have had inclinations to many more.
But I cannot ever remember wishing to be an engineer.
I always felt that your world was a world quite beyond
me. I admired it profoundly, but I admired it from
afar, as the ignoramus admires the expert.

Most professions, it seems to me, are empirical things
and deal largely in speculations and generalities. The
business of a lawyer, for example, is to give practical
application to general principles, but he is not dealing
with an exact science. No legal doctrine is really precise in its application. The work of a doctor, too, must
be largely experimental. As for the politician, the terms
he uses can never be accurately defined—that is part
of the fun of politics. Therefore in nearly every profession you have faddists and theorists. But the engineer
is wholly different. He has to deal with hard facts.
He knows that if he is not exactly right in his calcula-
tions he will be exactly wrong. That gives his mind, I
think, a clearness and precision which is not common in
other walks of life. I have had the good fortune to
know a fair number of eminent engineers, and I have

[1]*Engineering Institute of Canada Dinner. Montreal. 15th June, 1937.*

195

always been struck by the masculine firmness of their intelligence. There are no vague patches, no loose ends in their methods of thought.

Your profession has always been the foundation of every civilised society. You provide the basis, the physical basis, which makes government possible. That was so in the ancient monarchies of the East, and especially in ancient Egypt. There have not been many greater engineers in history than the Egyptians. The Greeks, it is true, were no engineers. They were interested more in the human mind than in the physical conditions of life. But they had to borrow a physical basis from their predecessors, and without these predecessors there would have been no Greek civilisation. When you come to the Romans, the real makers of the world as we know it, we find that they were above all things a race of engineers. The Roman roads, the Roman aqueducts, the Roman bridges still stand to-day in the Old World as a memorial of a people who based their society firmly on engineering science.

Here in Canada the engineer is faced with the same kind of problem as the Romans. In the Old World to-day I think one might say that nature has been largely conquered by the engineer. He has constantly to adapt and extend his conquests to meet new needs, but the initial problems have been solved. But here in this vast Dominion you have still the same kind of problem to face as the Romans had. You have to conquer space, and you have to adapt landscape to human needs. Your profession must always be a matter of expansion and pioneering, and therefore a living profession. You have already great engineering achievements to your credit; your transcontinental railways and your harnessing of water-power are among the miracles of applied science. But, the conquest of wild nature in Canada has only begun. I am convinced that in the future you will have still greater achievements to your credit. The future of the British Commonwealth, as I am never tired of declaring, depends largely upon applied science, and now, when the old days of territorial expansion are over, it is the engineer who is the principal empire-builder.

May I be permitted to say one word on a subject which concerns us deeply in Britain, and which, even in Canada, is not without its importance? The beauty and dignity of its landscape are among the chief assets of any nation. At home, in a small, closely settled country, this beauty must be carefully preserved, and it is most necessary to keep the balance between the aesthetic and the utilitarian interests. The secret and subtle loveliness of the English countryside can be speedily ruined if the only consideration is utility. Now it is very easy to be pedantic on this question. I have no sympathy with the point of view which sees in every modern development a menace to natural beauty. Nature has a wonderful power of absorbing human inventions. When railways were first started in England there was a loud outcry that the beauty of the countryside was gone. It was a foolish outcry, for the countryside has absorbed the railways and made them part of it. The same, I have no doubt, will be true of the great arterial motor-roads of the future. Take an achievement like the Forth Bridge. I remember in my boyhood how people declared that such a bridge would ruin the amenities of the Firth of Forth. The opposite has proved to be true. These great piers, with the sea at their feet and the Highland hills as their background, have enormously added to the picturesqueness of Scotland, by bringing in the human touch, just as the Pyramids have added to the wonders of the Egyptian desert. In Switzerland the pylons marching down the mountain-side, carrying electric power, have not spoilt the Alps; on the contrary they have added to their grandeur by placing homely human interests in contrast to their immensity. It is necessary in these matters to get rid of shallow aesthetic fads and take a robust view of what constitutes the picturesque.

But at the same time the constructive powers of man must keep in some kind of harmony with nature. Even in a country like Canada, where you are dealing with nature in its wildest form, the engineer should be also something of the artist. I think the introduction of a human interest does not spoil, but rather dignifies, any landscape. For example, I find a real beauty in the West in the grain elevators—with their white domes and towers, which carry the eyes from the immense Prairie levels to the blue Prairie sky. I do not suppose there was any conscious artistic purpose in the building of these elevators, but the result is excellent.

There is one engineering question in which I think there should be a conscious artistic purpose, and that is bridges. Canada is a country of bridges, and the bridge is one of the most beautiful of human creations. I hope Canadian engineers will keep this in mind and will see that the bridges are adequate to the grandeur of the natural setting. Remember that this Dominion of ours is destined to be the playground of North America, and that those who visit us will demand beauty as well as usefulness.

Your profession has a high mission. You have in your hands the making of the material background of a great nation. You are the pathfinders, the road-makers, the cyclopean architects of a land whose horizons are not limited, and whose development no man can assess.

THE LAW[1]

M R. TREASURER, My Lords, Ladies and Gentlemen:—You have done me a great honour and a great kindness, for which I offer you my sincerest thanks. It delights me to be back again among lawyers, for I feel that I am renewing my youth. In the words of the Roman poet, I, too, have lived in Arcadia; I, too, have been a lawyer. Thirty-five years ago I was called to the English Bar, after having been ploughed once in my Bar Final, in company with a friend who is to-day one of the chief ornaments of the English Bench. I am, in a sense, a link with the past, for I was the last pupil of that great man, John Andrew Hamilton, afterwards Lord Sumner, before he took silk. I devilled occasionally for Sir Robert Finlay in the days when he was Attorney-General. On the advice of Lord Haldane I wrote a law book on that obscure topic the taxation of foreign income, which was for a good many years the only treatise on the subject. So, gentlemen, you will see that at one time in my life I was respectable.

Then I fell from grace. I left the pastoral uplands of the law for the lower levels of commerce, and in my future relations with Courts of Justice I had to content myself either with the insignificant position of the lay client, or the dullness of the jury box or the witness box, though so far I have escaped the garish and uncomfortable notoriety of the dock. But now I seem to have been forgiven my backsliding. Last summer I was made a Bencher of my old Inn, the Middle Temple;

[1]*Law Society of Upper Canada. Toronto. 21st February, 1936.*

199

to-day you have deeply honoured me by making me an honorary member of the Bar of Upper Canada.

But though I ceased to practise law I did not lose my interest in it. Once a lawyer, always a lawyer. At home, I have been accustomed to read the law reports in "The Times" before I read anything else in that paper, and, indeed, I should do the same thing to-day if I could only find the law reports in your admirable Canadian press.

The popular mind has always amused itself with ribaldry at our expense. There is a proverb of my own country of Scotland which runs something like this— "Hame's aye hame, as the Devil said when he found himself in the Court of Session." And I have heard the Latin tag *nemo repente fuit turpissimus*—"no one becomes very bad all at once"—translated "It takes five years to become a solicitor." Gentlemen, just as hypocrisy is the tribute which vice pays to virtue, so I regard this popular ribaldry as the tribute which folly pays to wisdom.

I have had many professions, but there is none for which I have a higher regard than the Law. For one thing I do not think any profession excels ours in its strict standard of honour. I do not think there is any profession, too, so free from petty jealousy or so ready to admire proved ability. And in these days there are few professions more difficult. Without doubt our bodies are fearfully and wonderfully made, and the doctors have an intricate task; and theological questions do not get easier as time goes on, so the clergy have a difficult task. But I am very sure that no other profession has harder problems than ours. We have to face the eternal paradox—that laws are made in their final form by Parliaments and Congresses—that is, by people not perfectly adapted for the task, with the result that experts have to spend their lives interpreting them. This task does not grow easier in these days of super-abundant legislation, when the lawyer has often to straighten out the tangle left by the legislatures. To-day, I fear, too many modern Acts of Parliament, at least in Britain, have, as someone has said, all the appearance of lucidity and all the reality of confusion. Well, a tough job keeps a man young and keeps his mind active. I am always struck with the enduring vitality of lawyers, and that is one reason why I say that in coming among you I am renewing my youth.

But gentlemen, we have one great consolation. I have heard an atheist defined as a man who had no invisible means of support. You have always an invisible means of support in the reflection that the law which you interpret is, with all its imperfections, the true cement of civilisation. Here in Canada, as in England, as in the United States, we have as a precious heritage that body of customs and principles which we know as the Common Law. Like the British Constitution, it is an organic thing, the growth of which never ceases. Like the British Constitution, too, it is largely unwritten. Blackstone's great work is an essay on the subject rather than a digest.

It is your business not only to interpret that body of doctrine, but to enlarge it and to adapt it to the needs of a changing world. Law, I think, should be regarded as an elastic tissue which clothes the growing body. That tissue, that garment, must fit exactly. If it is too tight it will split, and you will have revolution and lawlessness, as we have seen at various times in our history when the law was allowed to become a strait-waistcoat. If it is too loose it will trip us up and impede our movements. Law, therefore, should not be too far behind or too far ahead of the growth of society, but should coincide as nearly as possible with that growth. Therefore it is your duty not merely to interpret a body of doctrine, but in your interpretation to keep it in close touch with contemporary life. You can never be pedants, or you will not be good lawyers. It was a wise saying of Mr. Justice Oliver Wendell Holmes, that "the life of the law is not logic but experience."

The task of the lawyer to-day is an intricate one, but it is a living one. I have called the law the chief bond of civilisation. It is also one of the chief bonds which link the British Empire together. Many of you will remember that famous occasion eleven years ago in Westminster Hall, when the lawyers of Britain and the lawyers of the Empire and the lawyers of the United States met to pay homage to the rock whence they were hewn. It is also one of our chief ties with that great nation south of our four thousand miles of undefended frontier. Jeremy Bentham warned the United States to "shut their ports against the Common Law as they would against the plague," but happily the United States did not follow his advice. They made our Common Law their own law, and through a succession of eminent judges, beginning with Story and John Marshall, they built up on it the ground-work of their national life.

So, gentlemen, you have cause to be proud of your profession. You are assisting in providing and administering that rational code of conduct, that union of discipline and liberty, without which no society can be wholesome and no nation can live.

Mining and Metallurgy[1]

I AM delighted to be here to-night. I am also honoured, for I have no claim to be present in such a gathering of experts, and still less to address you. But I have always taken a special pleasure in meeting men who know their business, who are adepts in a highly technical craft, and that, beyond question, is the character of this gathering to-night. Also I may modestly claim a very genuine interest in your subject. I have the interest which my office compels me to have in everything which concerns the well-being of Canada. And I have the special interest that once, early in my life, I was compelled to turn my attention to mining problems. When I was in South Africa just after the South African war, we had to deal with the difficult question of the future of the great gold industry of the Rand, and I was forced to acquire at least a smattering of the subject. Those were difficult days, for the South African mining industry became a party question at home, and we had the confusion which always attends an economic and scientific problem when it is brought into the heated world of politics. That, happily, is not your case to-day in Canada. By universal consent the future of this great Dominion depends largely upon your work.

That is no new thing in the world's history. Have you ever considered what an enormous part mining and metals have played in the progress of man? In a sense

[1]*Canadian Institute of Mining and Metallurgy Dinner. Ottawa. 19th March, 1936.*

they are the basis of history and of civilisation. The
stages of human progress are each linked with a special
metal, or at any rate with something dug out of the
earth. We began with the Stone Age; we advanced to
the Bronze Age, and then to the Iron Age. And we
either look back or look forward to a Golden Age.
What mankind calls treasure has always come out of
the ground, in the shape of jewels or silver or gold.
Had there been none of these things how different
history would have been! The passions of man and
the romance of life have all been interwoven with what
is hidden under the earth's crust.

I am not sure that one can easily define the purpose
of this Institute. It covers a vast ground. I have con-
sulted that racy little handbook "The Encyclopaedia
Britannica", but I did not gather much from it except
that there are an enormous number of metals and a
still more enormous number of minerals, and that
mining may be roughly divided into open-seam mining
and underground mining—which does not get one very
far. But whatever definition you choose it is perfectly
certain that Canada possesses most metals and a huge
assortment of minerals. Indeed, I understand that the
only thing you lack is manganese. In the few months
I have been here I have had the privilege of seeing
something of two mining areas—the gold and copper
mines in Northern Ontario, and the Asbestos mines of
Thetford, in the Eastern Townships. I hope during my
time in this country to see a great deal more; and that
will mean pretty extensive travelling, for you have
mineral wealth everywhere from the Great Lakes to
the Arctic Ocean, from the Prairies in the West to the
Atlantic coast. The great Laurentian Shield, which at
one time was thought to be a useless no-man's land,

now proves to be the roof of a gigantic treasure house.

It is a wonderful piece of good fortune for Canada that in these difficult days, when agriculture all over the world is in straits, and when normal industries are crippled, you should have found this new source of wealth, much of which can be as readily cashed as a Bank of England note. Thirty years ago no one would have dreamed of it; twenty years ago you were still fumbling for the lock.   It is a gift from Providence which has come unexpectedly out of the void, and of which we have only just begun to scrape the edges.

Let me give you a reminiscence. In the beginning of the year 1903, Mr. Joseph Chamberlain, who was then Colonial Secretary, came out to South Africa and delivered some admirable speeches, most of which I heard. At that time he was beginning to dream of a great Imperial economic federation, which a few months later he expounded to the world in his famous Tariff Reform scheme. I remember especially one of his speeches, when he argued that one notable feature of the Empire was that economically the Dominions were complementary. He instanced South Africa, which, he said, was probably the richest mineral area on the globe, but which could never be much of an agricultural country. He instanced Canada, which he said had the most wonderful soil on earth, but was wholly without minerals. How rash, gentlemen, is the business of prophecy!

Mining in South Africa has long passed from a speculation to an industry. The reef on the Rand has been traced and mapped for hundreds of miles and many mining companies can calculate years ahead to four places of decimals their costs and their profits, the only variable quantity being the price of gold. So far as I can judge the same thing is becoming true of Canada, except that you have a better prospect of happy surprises. There is every reason to believe that this land of ours is the richest mineral area on earth, and it is very certain that our grandchildren's grandchildren will not exhaust its possibilities. You have brought to your task the most up-to-date business methods, and you are using every new development in chemical and mechanical science. Mining is no longer a gamble, except in its first stage; it speedily becomes a highly organised business and an exact science.

There is one feature about your mining development which especially pleases me. In most mining areas—certainly in South Africa—the prospector, the man who did the pioneering work, did not reap the fruits of his labour. That was left to the capitalist who came after him, and who never stirred from his office chair. But here not only has the prospector often made the big money, but he has stuck to it—we have all many instances in our minds. But the old type of prospector whom I knew in my youth has, I fear, gone for ever— the simple fellow who worked by rule of thumb, who lived a life of desperate chances, and who went about his business with a gun in one pocket and a bottle of whiskey in the other. That picturesque figure is no more. The new type of prospector has—must have— more than a smattering of science. He gets to his prospecting grounds, not by canoe or by dog-team or by back-packing, but by air. He probably communicates with his superiors by wireless. And the contents of his pockets are not alcohol and lethal weapons, but a sheaf of air photographs!

But let no one say that romance can ever go out of

the business. There will always be romance when you are dealing with the unknown. When science has done all it can there will remain the human factor, the need of patience, the need of boldness, the willingness to take chances, that instinct which can never be set down in cold black and white. Mining will always remain an adventure. Indeed, the more it progresses the more the miraculous element will appear. Gold is a fairly obvious thing when you find it in the shape of dust or nuggets, but when you extract it from rock that looks like nothing so much as a bit of frozen haggis, then you work a marvel and a miracle. The more highly organised and scientific the business becomes, the more, to my simple mind, it takes on the character of a fairy tale. When I look at the methods of modern mining my feelings are very much those of the Highland minister who journeyed to London to visit the great Exhibition of 1851. When he returned he preached a sermon on the subject, which concluded as follows:— "As my eye wandered around these glassy domes, as it passed from nave to transept and back again from transept unto nave, then, my friends, was I filled with solemn thoughts—of the greatness of God and man's intellectual superiority."

MEDICINE

1[1]

I AM delighted to be present on this occasion, but I
am not sure that I have any business to be here. I
am still more doubtful as to whether I have any right
to address you, for I do not believe, if you searched this
country far and wide, you would find anyone more
deplorably ignorant of the sacred art of healing than
myself. I have shared, of course, like other mortals, in
the beneficent activities of your profession, but what
they did to me, and why, has always been one of
Allah's mysteries! Yet in a sense I have had much to
do with you for, as Member of Parliament for the
Scottish Universities for eight years, I represented a
considerable part of the medical faculty of Britain.
So, if I am profoundly ignorant of medicine, I have
every cause to be appreciative of its practitioners.

Since I came to Canada I have been greatly impressed by the high standing of your profession. Of
course, I knew it before, for at home your great medical
schools, like McGill and Toronto, have long been
famous. But I had not quite realised until I came to
Canada that you Canadian doctors were really the
medical "shock troops" of this continent. The great
American medical schools, I understand, such as Johns
Hopkins at Baltimore, and some of the chief clinics,
are largely manned by Canadians, and everywhere in
the United States a Canadian doctor has a position of
special prestige. I have been told—I need hardly say
by a fellow countryman—that you occupy in the States

[1]*Ontario Medical Association. London, Ont. 27th May, 1936.*

very much the position that a Scotsman does in England.

But what even an ignoramus like myself can do is to pay his tribute to your profession. I believe, if you polled the people of any country to-day as to what is the loftiest of all callings you would get the same answer. It would be the calling of medicine. There is no other which makes greater demands on the head and the heart, no other in which these demands are more gallantly met. The great Hippocratean Oath, now more than twenty centuries old, has set a high moral standard. Medical research does not patent its results, but at once makes them public for the benefit of all humanity. I have been fortunate enough in my time to know a good many great men, whom I deeply respected, and at the very top of the list I should put certain doctors. I remember I once saw Lord Lister in his old age, and I thought his face the most beautiful I had ever seen, with its gravity and simplicity and gentleness, and its air of serene meditation. It was the face of a conqueror, of a happy warrior who

> "Born to walk in company with pain
> And fear and blood-shed, miserable train,
> Turns his necessity to glorious gain."

I can imagine no worthier and no happier life than that of a great physician or great surgeon whose mind is kept bright and keen by constant thought, but in whose thinking there is none of the self-absorption of the pedant, since his powers are devoted to the practical work of mercy and humanity.

To keep the mind bright and keen—that is the eternal problem in every human occupation, and in its solution Associations such as yours, and a conference such as this, must play a distinguished part. For consider.

Take the profession of the law. Law, except within narrow limits, is not a progressive and a developing science. It is a body of rules which are occasionally altered and amplified by statutes, but which in substance remain the same for each generation of lawyers. A practising lawyer is always learning, no doubt, but he is not compelled, apart from his cases, to be constantly studying his subject. Very different is the case of the doctor, especially the general practitioner, who, I am sure you will agree, is the foundation stone of the whole profession. A busy doctor has his day filled with a variety of cases which he treats according to the knowledge and skill which he possesses; but he must constantly be adding to that knowledge and skill, for daily the work of research and experiment is adding to the doctor's equipment. If he is a conscientious man, he dare not get out of touch with the latest developments. He owes that duty to his patients. He cannot afford to treat a case by antique methods when new and better methods are available. And he owes that duty to himself. If he is worthy of his calling he must keep his mind bright and keen, he must keep in touch with a swiftly developing and intricate science to prevent his intelligence from ossifying in a maze of routine.

That must always be a difficult task. How is a busy man, whose days are crowded with urgent duties, to find time, to find the mental vitality, to read the latest medical books and the latest medical journals, and to keep abreast of that huge forward movement in his science, to which every civilised country is contributing? Here comes in the value of an Association like yours, of a convention like this. It brings the practising doctor in touch with his fellows. It enables him to exchange ideas, to hear from specialists the results of their work, and to furbish up all the weapons in his armoury.

May I add one last word as a tribute from a man of letters? Your skill has enriched our literature. Samuel Pepys, you remember, was, in his own phrase, "cut for the stone" in early life, and thereby given many years of fruitful and happy work, with enormous benefit to literature and to the public service. I often think with sadness how great the difference would have been in the life of many great writers if the medical science of their day had been more advanced. If, for example, Sir Walter Scott in early middle age could have been operated on for gall stones, twenty years might have been added to his life. If Thomas Carlyle could have been treated for duodenal ulcer, his days would not have been increased, for he lived to be a very old man, but his temper would have been enormously improved. But I am thinking especially, in my tribute, of how much the busy doctor has contributed to literature itself. I would take only two examples, an Englishman and a Scotsman, both of the same name. Sir Thomas Browne of the seventeenth century produced in his *Religio Medici*, and other books, masterpieces of English prose. Dr. John Brown in the last century, who wrote *Rab and his Friends* and a multitude of other delightful essays, was one of the glories of modern Scottish literature. If I may take an example from our own days and from my own friends, Lord Moynihan was not only a master of the spoken word, but one of the most widely read men I have ever met. And Lord Dawson of Penn, in the illness of the late King, was the author of those beautiful messages, during the last hours, which the world will long remember. A great doctor, therefore, can keep his mind bright and keen, not only by keeping abreast of medical science, but by maintaining his interest in humane letters.

MEDICINE

2[1]

IT IS a privilege to meet you all here to-day. I only
wish it had been possible for me to show you some
hospitality. But this is the season when Government
House is shut up and we are sojourning in Quebec; so
you must take the will for the deed. I am especially
glad to greet a society which embraces in its membership all Canada. I am the last to deny the value of the
local society and the provincial society, but I do not
think it possible to emphasize too highly the value of
an all-Canada association, for it reminds us that we
are not only nine provinces but a single and indivisible
nation.

Since I came to Canada I have on many occasions
paid tribute to the medical profession in the Dominion.
It has produced outstanding figures in medical science
whose fame has gone throughout the world. To-day in
Canada we have doctors and surgeons who have done
great work in research. We have given famous doctors
to Britain and famous doctors to the United States.
But I am thinking not only of what we might call the
grandees of the profession, but of the ordinary members
who throughout Canada to-day are performing faithfully the most arduous duties in the face of great difficulties and for very little reward. In some of the
drought areas of the Prairies last autumn I found
doctors, often with a brilliant college record behind
them, surrendering professional ambitions for the day-

[1]*Canadian Medical Association. Ottawa. 24th June, 1937.*

to-day work of relieving pain and sickness in poverty-stricken districts where the only recompense was the consciousness of faithful service. We in Canada have every cause to be proud of our outstanding figures, but we have every cause, also, to be proud of our rank and file.

To-day every sane man must be a devotee of peace, for most of us, except the very young, have had some personal knowledge of the terrible consequences of war. Heaven forbid that I should minimise these terrors; the best guarantee of peace is that the world should remember them. But great though the toll of war is, if you will look back through history you will find that the toll of disease is far greater. Man is a septic animal and if he is given a chance he poisons himself and his neighbours. In history we find that the loss of life by plague has always been infinitely greater than the losses on the battlefield. The plague in ancient Athens destroyed far more than the Peloponnesian War. In the Crusades it was not the deaths in the field that depleted Europe, but the leprosy which was brought back from the East. In the Thirty Years' War in Germany it was pestilence and not battle that wrought the worst devastation. In Napoleon's attack upon Russia, the chief losses on both sides were also from disease. In the Franco-German War in 1870 the small pox in Germany, which followed, killed more men by far than France lost on the battlefields. I would remind you, too, of the American Civil War, where two men died of disease for every one who fell in the field, of the British losses from enteric in the South African War, and of the terrible mortality from influenza throughout the world at the end of the Great War. Supposing we had tomorrow universal peace assured for all time, there would be little increased security for human life. If you want further information on this subject read Dr. Zinsser's brilliant book on "Rats, Lice and History." The true life-savers are the doctors and not the pacifists.

To-day, with a more closely settled and a more closely connected world, more is demanded from your profession than ever. With every advance of civilisation the problem of fighting disease becomes more complex. We have had great triumphs, as, for example, in our struggle with malaria, but with every triumph new problems seem to arise. Take, for example, yellow fever. It exists in West Africa, but happily it has not yet crossed that continent. But if, through modern communications, it should reach East Africa and spread thence to India and the Far East, we might have a repetition on a greater scale of the plagues of the Middle Ages. That is an example of a tremendous problem before preventive medicine.

And the problem is not less great in the long-settled lands. Our modern industrial civilisation has raised a host of new conundrums which your profession has to face daily. There again you have won great triumphs such as the lowering of infant and maternal mortality. But the problem before our health services never ceases. The organisation of your profession has become as complicated as the organisation of a great army. We have to see to the care of school children, the provision of pure milk, and a wiser and more nutritious diet. In our industries we have the problem of industrial fatigue, and in every calling we have the problem of nerve strain, of which we are only beginning to understand the rudiments. The work of preventive medicine is not merely the control of epidemics, but the laying of the foundation of a healthy society. If, as seems

probable, the population of the old countries is likely
to decline, we must at any rate make certain that the
smaller population of the future shall be a healthy
population. Never before in history, I think, has the
work of the doctor been so closely allied to the work of
the statesman.

That is one great side of your work. There remains
the fight with one or two major diseases. You have
done wonderful work in the case of tuberculosis, but
that is a war in which there is no discharge, for modern
life perpetually reproduces the conditions which en-
courage the disease. Everywhere to-day, too, research
work is being done in connection with cancer, that most
terrible of scourges, and there is good hope that with
increasing knowledge we may find new preventive and
curative methods. There is one thing worth remembering. We have done so much in recent years to reduce
mortality in the diseases of early life that the diseases
of later life, such as cancer, will bulk more prominently,
and statistics, which may have a depressing appearance,
should not mislead us into pessimism. There is another
malady in connection with which I should like to see a
determined campaign. The various rheumatic diseases
in England account for more lost working days than
any other single complaint. I understand that in
Canada, as in the United States, the thing is as much a
scourge as at home, and I hope that the medical profession here will give it serious attention. Here is a
disease where medical research has the most direct
bearing upon our economic welfare.

I offer you these few remarks as a very amateurish
student of your work, but as a profound admirer. May
I say one last word? We live in a world which is so
cumbered with difficult problems that there is a tend-

ency to look for short cuts in everything, some easy
panacea, some simple road to prosperity. We see it in
politics, where there are too many windy theories. We
see it in economics, where the fallacious short-cut has
so many votaries. You have to fight the tendency in
your own profession. There is always an inclination in
the ordinary man to forsake science for what I might
call magic. You have to fight the quack, just as the
statesman has to fight the theorist, and the economist
the charlatan. That is a humane and honourable duty,
for there is nothing crueller than to mislead mankind
by false hopes. In your profession you must keep an
open mind, that disinterested curiosity which leads to
new discoveries. But at the same time you must have
an honest mind, a mind which is a stern devotee of
sound reason. The hope for humanity does not lie in
flashy short-cuts, but in a patient following of the path
of clear thought and honest labour. Do you remember
a passage in *The Pilgrim's Progress?*—"Some have
thought," says Bunyan, "that there might be a passage
forthwith to their Father's house with no more hills
and valleys to go over, but the Way is the way, and
let that suffice". The Way is the Way, and there is no
shirking it. It may be long and difficult, but it gets
there in the end.

Medicine

3[1]

I AM very sensible of the honour you have done me in
making me an Honorary Fellow of your Royal
College of Physicians and Surgeons.

I have already had occasion to pay tribute—the
tribute of the outside spectator—to the high quality of
your profession in Canada, and to the prestige which it
enjoys on the American Continent. Here in Canada
you are in a wonderful position for you hold, it seems
to me, the strategic vantage ground in medical studies
on this Continent. You draw from England and Scotland—that I suppose is your main influence. You also
draw from France, and you have the great avenue which
joins you to the United States. You can never be
isolated; you will always be stimulated by fresh currents
of thought from many quarters. I cannot forget that
the greatest doctor I have ever known was a Canadian,
Sir William Osler.

And the memory of Osler leads me to remark how
interesting it is for a student of literature, such as
myself, to see how a great doctor can add to the technique of his profession a strong interest in humane
learning. Osler was one of the most widely cultivated
men I have ever known, a true scholar in other depart-
ments than medicine. The other day there died in
England an old friend of mine, Lord Moynihan, who
was of the same type, and who was incidentally, one of

[1]*Annual Dinner of the Royal College of Physicians and Surgeons
of Canada. Ottawa. 31st October, 1936.*

the greatest masters of the spoken word I have ever known. I have just been reading Dr. Harvey Cushing's "Note Book of a Surgeon in the Great War." I cannot imagine a more powerful argument for the abolition of war than his study of it from the point of view of a brain surgeon. What I want to say about that book is that it is so admirably written that it would be a credit to any man whose sole profession was letters. As the work of a busy surgeon it is an extraordinary performance in its mastery of sound English prose. But I am bound to say also that I have just read Dr. Cushing's Foundation lecture, published in the Foundation Volume of the Montreal Neurological Institute, and spent my time puzzling out, from my knowledge of Greek, the innumerable compounds beginning with *psycho* and *neuro*. My respect for Dr. Cushing became greater than ever, for it is not everyone who can write both what is brilliantly lucid and brilliantly obscure.

One might compare the duties of a doctor with those of a soldier, but it would be a very special kind of soldier. The ordinary battalion officer has a plain task before him, for he is under orders and need not trouble himself about the higher questions of strategy and tactics. He has his day-to-day task and that suffices. But the doctor is not only faced with a multitude of urgent duties, but he has to keep abreast of a rapidly developing science, for he owes it to his patients to bring to bear upon their cases the latest scientific developments. It is as if a battalion commander in action had, in addition to his normal duties, the business of understanding in detail the policy of his Commander-in-Chief.

Your profession, therefore, will always have its dual function. It has the duty of research and experiment in the quest for truth, the enlargement of its sphere of knowledge. And it has also the duty of applying its existing body of knowledge to the daily tasks of alleviating pain and misery. It has the functions of a General Staff, and also the functions of what I might call the Q. side of an army. I have lately been on an extensive tour in the Prairie Provinces and have visited many of the outland districts. There I have been enormously struck with the work of your profession in all its branches. I have found doctors with huge areas to cover, leading a life as hard as that of any pioneer. I have found little stricken townships where small hospitals contrive to function gallantly with slender staffs and narrow means. I have met men who at college had taken high honours and who began their Prairie practice with hopes of being able to continue some branch of research and visions before them of further training in London or Berlin or Vienna. These visions are now things of the past, and they have settled down to the hard day-to-day task of relieving suffering, putting behind them their professional ambitions in the interests of common humanity. They had no reward— no material reward—only their labours, only the consciousness of a difficult duty faithfully performed. I have never met men whom I have more sincerely respected. Your profession in Canada has won international repute for its contributions to medical science. But do not let us forget the other side; the hundreds of men who are labouring faithfully and obscurely in the remoter districts, maintaining the highest traditions of one of the noblest and most unselfish of human vocations.

We are all inclined sometimes to speculate about the future. One often hears it said that we have got on terms with the chief diseases which afflicted our forefathers; but that the advance of civilisation will always bring new ailments. We may have mastered the old epidemics, like small pox, the plague, and typhoid; but the strain of modern life has brought a multitude of new afflictions, both of the body and the mind. Now I think we are wrong if we imagine that our ancestors had only straight-forward physical ailments, and suffered little from subtler things. If you will read the memoirs of two centuries ago you will find constant references to complaints which were clearly neurotic— the green sickness, for example, from which young women suffered in the eighteenth century, the "melancholic" habit from which stalwart figures like Oliver Cromwell were not exempt. If I may speak as an historian, it seems to me that very few of the great figures of history were what might be called healthy and normal people. Most of them did their work under grave physical handicaps for which there was then no medical relief. You have Julius Caesar with his mysterious epilepsy; you had Robert the Bruce with a painful skin disease; you had Cromwell with some kind of spleen trouble; you had Walter Scott with gall-stones—I think I could find a pathological side to almost every famous historical figure. These men did their work to a very constant accompaniment of pain.

My friend, Colonel Lawrence of Arabia, used to maintain to me that bodily pain was a real mental stimulant, and that half his inspiration in Arabia came from the fact that he was wrestling all the time with pain and weakness. I do not know what scientific basis there may be for that view, but I think we may take it as true that in the past some of the chief work of the world, both in action and thought, has been performed to the accompaniment of pain.

Today much of that pain would be relieved. Of that I think there can be no question. We have no doubt acquired certain intricate and mysterious medical problems of our own; but the more obvious things we can relieve by operation or treatment. Now I cannot but feel that in this there is a clear gain. Pain may be a stimulant to the mind, but it is also a source of confusion and bewilderment. It blurs the perspective, obscures the sense of proportion and disturbs the balance. If we can get rid of it we prepare the way for a more level judgment and a saner perspective. I feel that that is one great gain on which we can pride ourselves. Our public problems to-day are intricate as perhaps they have never been before, and what above all is needed is a steady balance and a stalwart common sense. We need far less the inspirations of genius than patience, equanimity and sound judgment in the ordinary man. If the advance of medical science can provide this, as I believe it can, then it is contributing something of incalculable value to the peace and comfort of the world.

I AM always happy, gentlemen, in the company of your profession. For two months this autumn I was very much in medical society, for I had a rest and a "cure" in a famous clinic among the Welsh mountains. I arrived in England in the summer rather weary, and after a strenuous fortnight of interviews and speeches and discussions I was dog-tired, so Lord Dawson promptly despatched me to a place where I was under discipline and had nothing to do except to get well. It was an experience of which I can only say that I enjoyed every moment, and I especially enjoyed the company of the distinguished doctors and specialists attached to the institution.

So I came to reflect a good deal upon medical science, and I venture to offer you a few of these reflections to-night. When I observed the careful, patient and precise curative work going on around me I realised how well-deserved was the reputation of your profession. That reputation has been high ever since the time of Hippocrates and Galen, and it has never been higher than to-day. If you will look at the statute of Henry VIII which confirmed the Letters Patent establishing the Royal College of Physicians in England, you will find that none were "to be suffered to exercise and practice physic but only those persons that be profound, sad and discreet, groundedly learned and deeply studied in physic." I am very certain that the company

1Ottawa Medical Society Dinner. 29th October, 1938.

here to-night is profound and discreet and deeply learned, but I am glad to think that it is not sad.

Not only has your profession always been admired, but it has been always popular. A proof is that it is the subject of many jokes. Human nature does not joke about anything which it fears or dislikes. It would be possible to make an amusing anthology of gibes at the sacred art of healing. There is, for example, the sentence of Rousseau—"Live according to nature and never mind the doctors. That will not prevent you dying, but it will prevent you dying more than once." The other day in a life of Sydney Smith I came on one that was new to me. He was staying in a country house at a shooting party, and after the day's shoot an eminent physician came in in a bad temper. "I shot scandalously," he said, "at the last stand. I hardly killed any birds." "My dear fellow," said Sydney Smith, "why didn't you prescribe for them?" That kind of ribaldry is the homage which ignorance pays to skill, skill for which it has a real affection. It is a common phrase, "a beloved physician". Did you ever hear people talk of a beloved accountant or a beloved electrical engineer?

At the same time, medical science has always had a certain aura of mystery about it. In the Middle Ages a doctor was not a man to be trifled with, for he had uncanny powers at his call. He might be a good man but he was not supposed to be always too good a Christian. You remember the description of the doctor in Chaucer's *Canterbury Tales*—"His studie was but litel on the Bible". A physician was a master not only of strange drugs but of spells and incantations.

Those days are long gone, but there is still a certain atmosphere of mystery about your craft. The ordinary man may have a smattering of law, but as a rule he knows very little about medicine. Now that is both a good and a bad thing. It is a good thing, for it makes sensible people put themselves in a doctor's hands when they are sick, and do what he tells them, since they recognise their ignorance. It is a bad thing, for it opens the door to the quack and the charlatan.

So to-night I am going to make two suggestions to you, the suggestions of a layman, made with all deference and modesty. The first is this. I believe it would be an excellent thing if your profession saw that the ordinary public had some elementary instruction in the rudiments of medicine. It need not be deep. It need concern itself only with the most general principles, and it should be directed to the prevention of needless anxieties and false hopes. If, for example, it were firmly rooted in the popular mind that something out of a bottle or a tube will not cure cancer, then a good many quacks would go out of business. Again, long experience has made us pretty familiar with certain common ailments, but there appears to be a host of new diseases, mysterious affairs with which the ordinary man is completely unfamiliar, and which in consequence he dreads. *Omne ignotum* is not only *pro magnifico*, but also *pro horrifico*. I find in many quarters something very like panic when certain diseases are mentioned such as infantile paralysis and sleeping sickness and streptococcus infections. I believe that much could be done to steady the popular mind if your profession were prepared to give a little elementary instruction on such subjects.

My second suggestion can be put in a sentence of Plato written two thousand years ago. Here it is— "This is the greatest error in the treatment of sickness, that there are physicians for the body and physicians for the soul, and yet the two are one and indivisible." There is a profound truth in that saying. More and more to-day we realise the close inter-connection between mind and body. The nerves play a prominent part in most ailments, and in most cases the nerves represent a condition of mind. Hygiene and therapy should cover the whole area of human needs, and the doctor must have an eye to the spiritual as well as to the physical make-up of his patient. It is not enough to have specialists for mental diseases and specialists for physical diseases; the same man must in a sense be both. A good doctor should be—and indeed always has been—something of a psychologist. I remember hearing Lord Horder once say that the first text-book of medicine should be a primer of logic. And I personally should always distrust the psychologist who had not a considerable knowledge of medical science.

There, gentlemen, you have two of my reflections this autumn, in the intervals of being X-rayed and dieted among the Welsh hills.

IX
LITERATURE

RETURN TO MASTERPIECES[1]

A YEAR ago, in this very city, and to an audience
much the same as this, I made a plea for a catholic
taste in reading. I urged my hearers not to be too
academic in their selection, not to keep only to the
main roads of letters, but to amuse themselves in the
by-paths. I still adhere to that view. It is enormous
fun to browse at large over the wide domain of literature, and one may pick up some surprising treasures in
unlikely places. In the last two centuries, for example,
there have been many minor poets who wrote in the
Scots vernacular, most of them uncommonly bad. But
even in the worst of them you can find an occasional
verse of singular beauty.

Let me give you two other illustrations. There was a
fifteenth-century English poet called John Lydgate, a
disciple of Chaucer and one of the prosiest of God's
creatures. But Lydgate in a love poem could write a
verse like this—

> And as I stoode myself alloone upon the Nuwe Yere night,
> I prayed unto the frosty moone, with her pale light,
>   To go and recomaunde me unto my lady dere.
> And erly on the next morrowe, kneling in my cloos
> I preyed eke the shene sonne, the houre whane he aroos,
>   To goon also and sey the same in his bemys clere.

Listen to this also. It is on the subject of Lady Jane
Grey—

> Like her most gentle, most unfortunate,
> Crown'd but to die—who in her chamber sate
> Musing with Plato, though the horn was blown,
> And every ear and every heart was won,
> And all in green array went chasing down the sun.

[1]*Convocation Hall. Toronto. 24th November, 1937.*

229

That is the work of Samuel Rogers, a banker and a minor poet at the beginning of last century, whom Lord Rosebery has described, not unfairly, as a "hedgehog soul".

But to-night I want to emphasize the other side. The back-waters have their charm, but we must not forget the main stream, the central tide of poetry. My plea is for a return to a proper respect for, and a more intimate knowledge of, the great masterpieces, the work of the primary creative minds.

I propose to take the narrower definition of poetry. Poetry and prose are not antithetical words, for there may be great poetry in great prose. The French word *poésie* is frequently applied to prose compositions. You remember Sir Philip Sidney's words, "It is not rhyming and versifying that maketh poesy. One may be a poet without versing, and a versifier without Poetry." The true differentiation is between prose on the one hand and verse or metre on the other. But for our purpose to-day I propose to take poetry in the narrower sense, as involving some kind of ordered rhythmical pattern— what, if printed in the ordinary prose fashion, would lose something of its effect.

How shall we define a masterpiece, a classic? I suppose by its enduring charm, for age does not wither it, and by its universal appeal, which is not limited by race or nationality. To take only the great literatures, I mean by master poets Homer and Aeschylus and Sophocles; I mean Lucretius and Horace and Virgil; I mean Dante; I mean Racine and Corneille and Victor Hugo; I mean Chaucer and Shakespeare; Milton and Dryden; Wordsworth and Coleridge; Shelley and Keats; Matthew Arnold (though some of my hearers may differ from me), and Tennyson and Browning.

My plea is timely, I think, for to-day there is a tendency to forget about the masters, or to treat them disrespectfully. Too many of our contemporaries are like impudent little boys who amuse themselves by making faces at their betters. For this fashion there are several reasons. One is that to-day, while there is an inordinate number of clever writers, there is a remarkable and admitted dearth of great ones, both in English and in French literature. I am old enough to remember Tennyson's death. When I was a young man we had Swinburne and Robert Bridges alive in England, and Hardy and Meredith and Ruskin. Less than two years ago with Kipling died one of the last of the write.s of the larger stature. It is the same in France since the death of Proust and Anatole France. There may be stupendous geniuses growing up in the world, but they have not yet revealed themselves. We live in a day of small things. We fail in respect to the bigger things, because we are not producing them.

Another reason is the impatience, the natural impatience, of our somewhat disintegrated youth. This inevitably tends to a kind of sansculottism. I am not inclined to describe these young men in the words of the poet as

Feeble and restless youths, born to inglorious days.

Feeble is not the right word for them, and there is both pathos and promise in their disquiet, but they are indubitably restless.

In their attitude to the great things of the past they have what is called in the jargon of to-day, an inferiority complex, with its inevitable converse, a superiority complex. They are perturbed by the spectacle of something beyond their compass and find consolation in affecting to despise it, like some Greek of the decadence who chipped off the nose of a marble statue in order to make the Goths laugh. We have many cases to-day of an easy notoriety won by belittling great reputations. If you declare that Wordsworth as a poet was much inferior to some hitherto unknown person called Snooks, whom you have discovered, you make people stop to listen to you and you flatter your own vanity, for you know that while you are a long way from Wordsworth, you are pretty much on a level with Snooks. So the attitude of these unfortunates to the masterpieces in poetry is very much that described in the first lines of Browning's "Grammarian's Funeral"—

> Let us begin and carry up this corpse,
> Singing together.

They are like the French Romantics at the beginning of last century whose cry was "Qui nous délivra des Grecs et des Romains?"—Who will deliver us from the tyranny of the great classics? They want to get rid of them, to bury them ceremonially, for their calm perfection is a standing reproach.

There is a third reason, and a more honourable one. Those iconoclasts are not as a rule very learned, and therefore they have not the just perspective which is given by a wide acquaintance with great literature. But they *feel* acutely. They are highly sensitive to the difficulties and discontents of our time. They demand in poetry a personal and topical note, an immediate contemporary appeal. They see no value in what they call the poetry of "escape". So we find in our younger school of poets at home two interesting features. We live, they say, in a mechanical age, so they crowd their verse with technological phrases and exult in the complexities of machinery. Again, they say, we live in an age of social unrest, and unless a poet has on this point a direct message, a new gospel of social regeneration, he is a mere cumberer of the ground.

I feel a good deal of sympathy with their view. No great poetry can be deaf to the "still sad music of humanity". It cannot ignore what Wordsworth calls—

> the fierce confederate storm
> Of sorrow barricadoed evermore
> Within the walls of cities.

It must have some gospel for mortal needs and mortal aspirations. But to ask from it a narrow political or economic faith is to wrong its majesty. What is proudly called "left-wing poetry" should often, to my mind, be more properly described as "half-baked poetry". Those writers, as Dr. Chalmers said of Thomas Carlyle, "prefer seriousness to truth", and they have the wrong definition of seriousness. Their ears are dulled by the rattle of machinery, and their perspective blurred by factory chimneys. They condemn the literature of escape, but in a true sense all good literature seeks escape, escape from the dust of the trivial, the partisan, the transient, to a clearer air and a wider landscape. I remember when I was very young that many elegant poets, like Austin Dobson, were concerned with fabricating pretty playthings in exotic forms of verse, like the French *rondeau* and *ballade*. A pleasant backwater, but one remote from the great tidal streams of poetry. But the poets of to-day are just as remote when, in cacophonous verse, they attempt the role of propagandists. The only difference is that their backwater is an uglier one, comparable not to a pleasant reach of the upper Thames, but to one of the dismal creeks on the Essex side of London, where scraps of rusty machinery litter the unlovely shores.

"Who will deliver us from the Greeks and Romans?" The answer is no one, if by the Greeks and Romans we mean the greater masterpieces of literature. They enshrine things permanent and universal. They have a largeness and rightness, both in thought and style, which no change in literary fashion can affect. They do not preach a specific creed; but, in Shelley's words, they "repeal large codes of fraud and woe". They dignify life because they link it with the eternal. They make the world at once more solemn and more sunny, brighter and more spacious—

Hesperus with the hosts of Heaven came,
And lo! Creation widen'd in man's view.

I would suggest to you two reasons why a people should live in close contact with masterpieces. The first concerns its character and its mind. There is a passage in the treatise which we call *Longinus on the Sublime* which is worth remembering. "It is not possible that men with mean and servile ideas and aims prevailing throughout their lives should produce anything that is admirable and worthy of immortality. Great accents we expect to fall from the lips of those whose thoughts are deep and grave." The converse of this is equally true, and it is with that converse that we are concerned. "Great accents", "thoughts deep and grave" in the literature of a nation will produce gravity and dignity both in the character and in the speech of the ordinary citizen.

Let me give you examples. Take the Greeks of the fifth and fourth centuries before Christ. Their thought and speech were interpenetrated with the poetry of Homer. They quoted him as our fathers used to quote the Bible. Plato, who objected, you remember, to poets as a class, manages to quote Homer more than 150

times. Who shall say how much this influence determined the speech, the thought, and the character of
Athens in her great days?

Take the Irish peasantry. No one can go among
them without noting the curious beauty and elevation
of the speech of many old people who never had any
schooling in their lives. Where did they get it? Partly
from the offices of their Church, and partly from the
folk-tales and folk-poetry which an Education Department has not expelled from their memories.

Take our own people in Britain and throughout the
Empire. There is one masterpiece which for more than
three centuries has been their constant study—the
English translation of the Bible. It has influenced their
lives, it has dominated their thoughts, and it has
coloured their speech. I fear that to-day the Bible is
not read as it used to be. I leave the Churches to say
how this neglect may affect the soul of our nation, but
I am very certain that it will have a malign consequence
for our thought and speech. Familiarity with the noble
rhythms of the Authorized Version made the plain man,
in a moment of emotion, a great orator; I would instance
Sir Arthur Currie's address to the Canadian troops in
the crisis of April, 1918. It enabled an unlettered man
like John Bunyan to produce in his *Pilgrim's Progress* a
book which, apart from its other merits, is a well of
undefiled English. It gave the speech of our people,
gentle and simple alike, the Roman virtues of *gravitas*
and *pietas*. If the Bible should go out of the national
memory and its place be taken by the jargon of a crude
popular science, or the jingles and captions of popular
forms of entertainment, then what a fall would be
there, my countrymen!

As a last example I would take my own people of the

Scottish Border. There, ever since the days of John Knox, there has been a certain level of education. Two things were in the possession of everyone, the Bible and the Ballads. To have them in their memory meant that they had a treasure-house of great literature behind them, for the Ballads are often great literature. James Hogg, in his *Shepherd's Calendar*, has shown how real a thing the Bible was in the life of the Border peasant. He made it the lamp of his path, and at family prayers communed frankly with his Maker. He revered the Bible, but the spirit of critical independence was not absent, and he was under no blind bondage to its letter. Hogg tells us that he would stop his reading of it with the remark, "If it hadna been the Lord's will, that verse had been better left out". But its august visions and its noble prose gave dignity to his life. And from the ballads of the countryside he drew also a wild poetry. I have heard plain folk in the upper glens of Tweed and Ettrick use in their ordinary speech phrases and metaphors which were a key to a whole world of mystery and imagination. Sir Walter Scott knew this, and, as was said of him, he "made his kail with other men's groats". When he makes his peasants, Meg Merrilees and Edie Ochiltree and Jeanie Deans, speak with a moving eloquence, he is not romancing. He had heard such words in moments of high tension on the lips of the unlearned, and, though less commonly, we may still hear them to-day.

The second reason I would suggest for the study of masterpieces is a literary one. They give us a standard of values. Matthew Arnold, you remember, was fond of taking certain famous lines of poetry as touchstones, and using them to test the quality of work about which

he was in doubt. I think perhaps that he rather over-
did the practice. A single line or verse seems to me to
be too narrow a measure. It may do as a test of melody
or rhythm, but scarcely for the rarer qualities of poetry.

But Matthew Arnold's general principle is right.
Every lover of poetry should be also a critic if he is to
have full enjoyment of it, and the meaning of criticism
is simply intelligent comparison. That is to say, before
a man can be said to have developed a critical faculty
he must have read the masterpieces and have his
memory stored with good literature. It seems to me
that the chief defect of our criticism to-day is that the
critics are so ignorant. They have read so little that
they have no proper standards of comparison. Almost
every week they discover a masterpiece in prose or
verse. No doubt that is a proof of a friendly and
generous spirit, and it is a good deal better than a per-
petual *dénigration*. Tennyson, you remember, did the
same thing. I have been re-reading lately the letters of
Edward Fitzgerald, and I find that Tennyson was
almost too appreciative of the merits of his contemporaries. He discovered, for example, sublimity in
an epic called *Festus* by Philip James Bailey, produced
in the sixties of last century, a deplorable work which
is now deservedly forgotten. But, at the same time,
too much critical complaisance is a danger, for it
debases the critical currency. When we read that some
vast, shapeless, modern novel must rank among the
great masterpieces of fiction, let us test the judgment
by casting our minds back to the best of Balzac, to
The Heart of Midlothian, or to *Vanity Fair*, or to
Middlemarch. When we are told that some piece of
tortured obscurity in verse is unparalleled since Donne,
well, let us recall Donne, who is cited to-day more than

he is read. When some limp lyric is praised as "sheer beauty"—a favourite phrase of our critics—let us test it by "The Grecian Urn", or the best of Shelley or Landor. Only thus shall we keep our heads straight and our palates clean for true appreciation.

This intelligent comparison is especially important when we are dealing with work which enshrines the special and peculiar genius of a literature. I should define this genius in every case as a particular kind of simplicity which is untranslatable into any other form of speech. It is the last word in inevitability; alter a syllable and you spoil it. It is the thrill which is incommunicable by any other collocation of words. The high-coloured, the artificial, the elaborate, the rhetorical can be rendered easily enough in translation. You can get the quality of Demosthenes more or less in English, but not of Plato; of Apollonius Rhodius, but not of Homer; of much of Euripides, but very little of Aeschylus and Sophocles. Ovid and Lucan can be adequately translated, but scarcely Horace, and emphatically not Catullus and Virgil. You can reproduce Bossuet successfully in English, but not Pascal; Victor Hugo, but not François Villon or Racine.

This alembicated and distilled simplicity is to my mind the highest quality of literature, and, since it is indefinable, a thing which can be felt and not explained, we can only recognize it by the method of comparison, by using as a touchstone the great examples of it. To-day there is a good deal of bogus simplicity about. Our poets are inclined to think that they attain inevitability by letting their thoughts and impressions pour out in a congested mass, by opening their mouths, like Balaam's ass, for Providence to fill with words. But crudity is not simplicity. The simplicity of genius is achieved only by much searching and by a strenuous discipline. M. Jourdain, you remember, in Molière's play, *Le Bourgeois Gentilhomme*, was amazed to discover that all his life he had talked prose without knowing it. He was quite wrong; he never talked prose; for prose, in any serious sense, is an artistic construction—words, as someone has defined it, in the best order. Poetry, to continue the definition, is the best words in the best order, and the greatest poetry is the only possible words in the only possible order. You can shake up most of our modern simplicities in a hat, and the result would be just as good; with the great simplicities you cannot alter an inflection or a letter.

Turn to Shakespeare. I have always regarded the songs in the plays as the high-water mark of lyrical beauty. Their content is very simple—obvious, if you like; their music is far from elaborate. But attempt to put them in any other form and they will be either ridiculous or banal. Let us try. Here is "Sigh no more, Ladies", as rendered by Sir Arthur Quiller-Couch into the stilted language which we usually reserve for translations from the classics—

> I enjoin upon the adult female population, not once but twice, that there be from this time forward a total cessation of sighing. The male is, and has been, constantly addicted to inconstancy, treading the ocean and the mainland respectively with alternate feet.

Here is the greatest of them all, "O! Mistress Mine" in the debased speech of a Hollywood film—a little effort of my own—

> Huh! Sweetie, where you gettin' to?
> Your big boy's here and pettin' you,
>   And he's the guy that rings the bell.
> Say, kid, quit hikin' and sit nice,
> For shakin' feet don't cut no ice,
>   The goopiest mutt can tell.

Both, mark you, are faithful renderings; in both the trite thought is expressed with extreme simplicity; but it is the wrong kind of simplicity.

Take again almost the greatest lines which he ever wrote—

> We are such stuff
> As dreams are made on, and our little life
> Is rounded with a sleep.

There is nothing recondite in the thought. It has been a platitude since the days of the Book of Job. There is nothing recondite about the language. It is composed of short, simple words which we use every day. Wherein then lies the secret? Ah! that we cannot tell. The alchemy of genius has compounded those simple ingredients into something inimitable and immortal. It is a jewel, in the glow of which most of our shallow modern simplicities shrivel and fade.

Well, ladies and gentlemen, I have given you my text, and now I come to what old-fashioned preachers used to call the application. The object of this meeting to-night is to foster an interest in Canadian poetry. That purpose has all my sympathy, for it is on poetry that we must build the foundations of that distinguished contribution which I believe Canada is destined to make to the literature of the world. Poetry is the earliest and most natural expression of the spirit of man, for it represents primarily an instinct, whereas prose is a considered affair which demands a more elaborate background. Great verse, in Keats' words, can be left to a little clan, but prose belongs to a more complex society. Two centuries before the Greeks developed their wonderful prose Sappho was writing immortal lyrics, and still earlier Homer had produced immortal epics. Therefore, it seems to me, this land of ours which, though it has a long history behind it, is still fortunate to be in the making, must look to poetry as the primary expression of its natural culture. You have already produced good poets, and to-day I recognize with pride the reality of your poetic impulse.

I want to see that impulse create its own idiom. The weakness, I think, of the poetry hitherto produced by the overseas Empire is that it has been too apt to borrow its idioms from the home country. Australian poetry, for all its admirable vigour, has in the past been inclined, even in the case of Adam Lindsay Gordon, to put its new wine into old bottles, and to sing of an unconventional world in conventional jingles. The same thing was once true of South Africa, though it is less true to-day. Every part of the Commonwealth should have its own idiom, and I want to see Canada provide its special version, and not borrow it from elsewhere. The modes in which English poets have sung of the English tradition, and of the mellow English landscape, are not those best fitted for our prairies and forests and mountains and northern wilds, or for a young and adventurous people. Canada must make her own music. What is wanted, in the words of the Scriptures, is a "new song to the Lord".

But, at the same time, let us remember that great literature is one and indivisible. The master singers have an appeal which is permanent and universal, as real to us here as to ancient Athens and Rome, to the England of Elizabeth or the France of Louis XIV. No nation can cut itself off from the past. We must have a criterion of value, standards by which to test our ventures, an inspiration to link the new and old, the known and the unknown. Before a spearman can cast a spear he must have firm ground to stand on. If the fisherman is to make a good forward cast he must first make a good back cast. To hold up our heads in a new world it is advisable to have a patent of nobility from an old world. But enough of these mixed metaphors! The moral I would point is very simple. In a country like ours, where our task is to force audacious novelties into the bonds of art, we need especially the master-pieces, which do not date, and whose appeal is to all humanity. They will provide that austere canon to which our new idioms must conform if they are to endure; that eternal background which will at once inspire and dignify our own reading of life.

The French Tongue[1]

(La Langue Francaise)

JE ME sens très honoré d'être invité à vous rencontrer en cette occasion. Je veux tenter de vous parler en cette langue que vous avez pour but principal de conserver pure, et je compte que votre bonté vous rendra indulgents à mes multiples gaucheries. Tout homme sage, tout Ecossais en particulier, croit certainement que le mélange des races fortifie une nation. Le Canada a le bonheur de posséder deux des grandes traditions de l'Europe, la française et l'anglaise. Vous avez conservé votre langue, votre droit, votre religion, et votre culture si riche d'histoire, d'un si grand prix pour le Canada tout entier. Votre langue surtout est un bien précieux, car la langue et la littérature françaises constituent une richesse non seulement pour le Canada français mais encore pour le Canada anglais.

L'anglais est une belle langue et la littérature anglaise est belle. La langue anglaise a besoin d'être gardée avec sollicitude, car étant parlée dans l'univers entier, elle risque grandement d'être contaminée par toutes sortes d'influences. Vous vous souvenez sans doute d'un passage amusant du *Mariage de Figaro* de Beaumarchais, et qui n'est pas très respectueux:

"C'est une belle langue que l'anglais; il en faut peu pour aller loin. Avec *god dam*, en Angleterre, on ne manque de rien nulle part . . . Les Anglais, à la vérité, ajoutent par-ci par-là quelques autres mots en conversant; mais il est bien aisé de voir que *god dam* est le fond de la langue".

[1]*Congrès de la Langue Française. Quebec. June, 1937.*

Beaumarchais n'a pas dit toute la vérité. Depuis
quelques années, on a vu le public de France témoigner
une estime particulière à la littérature anglaise; ce sont
des érudits français qui ont rédigé quelques-uns des
meilleurs travaux sur les écrivains anglais.

Mais aujourd'hui c'est de votre langue que je viens
vous parler. Il y a longtemps que je m'intéresse au
parler et à la littérature du Canada français. Le
français que l'on parle chez vous, surtout à la cam-
pagne, est plein de beauté et de pittoresque, grâce aux
réminiscences historiques, aux locutions marines qu'y
ont laissées les voyages des premiers Français venus au
pays. Je regrette seulement de ne pas le mieux comprendre. La littérature canadienne-française suit la
grande tradition classique de France. On peut relever
les écrivains français qui ont influé sur elle à chaque
génération. Au siècle dernier, par exemple, on re-
trouvait chez Crémazie et Nelligan l'influence des
grands romantiques français. La poésie contemporaine,
celle de Paul Morin et de Robert Choquette, par exemple, s'inspire de modèles plus récents. Je suis particulièrement frappé de ce que l'influence française se
fait toujours sentir avec un certain retard au Canada.
Ce n'est jamais la dernière mode de France qui touche
nos écrivains canadiens-français. Victor Hugo, par
exemple, n'est plus très lu en France aujourd'hui mais
son influence me paraît encore vivante au Canada. Je
crois que ce retard est un avantage; il empêche nos
écrivains de n'être que de serviles copistes et leur permet
de donner à leurs oeuvres un tour spécial au Canada.

Depuis mon arrivée au pays j'ai parcouru avec
plaisir une bonne partie de la littérature canadienne-
française, guidé surtout par les oeuvres de mon ami,
Mgr Camille Roy, le grand seigneur de la littérature

canadienne. J'ai particulièrement admiré vos travaux
d'histoire et de poésie. Vous possédez le vrai sens his-
torique et vous êtes bien inspirés de compléter vos
annales. Vous vous êtes admirablement servis de votre
histoire régionale pour conserver cette suite entre le
passé et le présent qui constitue le fondement de la
force nationale. Votre poésie, qui exprime si bien
l'âme d'un peuple, m'a profondément intéressé. Mais
le Canada français ne fait que commencer son oeuvre
littéraire. Il réunit tous les éléments d'une grande
littérature—un peuple dont l'histoire est l'une des plus
romanesques qui soient, une paysannerie qui heu-
reusement a su rester proche du terroir et conserver ses
vieilles traditions. Je prévois que le Canada français
collaborera avec distinction à ces travaux de l'esprit qui
resteront toujours à la base de la civilisation véritable,
car il participe de deux grandes traditions, la française
et l'anglaise. Comme le chantait Octave Crémazie,
"Albion notre foi, la France notre coeur". J'exprime
aussi le désir que nous voyions un jour naître chez vous
quelque chantre du peuple comme le Robert Burns de
mon Ecosse, qui traduira l'âme nationale en vers im-
périssables. Vos "habitants" ont produit beaucoup
d'agréables chansons, mais n'ont pas encore trouvé leur
grand poète.

Mais la littérature saura bien se faire jour. Le vent
de l'inspiration souffle où il veut, personne ne peut le
diriger. Par contre, c'est de nous qu'il dépend de conserver la pureté du langage. La gloire de la langue
française repose sur sa pureté, sa précision, son exquise
clarté. Comme l'écrivait un critique du dixhuitième
siècle,—

"Elle est de toutes les langues la seule qui ait une
probité attachée à son génie."

Dans le monde contemporain, si agité, une langue qui n'est pas protégée par des frontières est exposée à bien des influences pernicieuses. Comme je l'ai déjà dit, je crois le français moins menacé que l'anglais, mais il est menacé tout de même. Je ne m'oppose pas aux néologismes, car il en faut dans un monde qui progresse rapidement. Je redoute davantage les atteintes à la construction, à l'*ordonnance* logique qui a toujours fait la gloire du français. Un peu d'*argot* même ne me déplaît pas, parce que la langue littéraire s'enrichit constamment d'apports populaires. Mais je tiens à ce que l'on respecte religieusement la construction, car c'est d'elle que dépend la clarté. Comme disait un grand critique français: "Ce qui n'est pas clair n'est pas français".

Les ennemis les plus dangereux de la langue ne se trouvent pas chez le peuple, mais parmi les pédants. Bien des sciences semblent se fabriquer un obscur jargon, farci de néologismes abstrus et de tours pesants. Elles manquent de la clarté qui devrait être le but principal de tout écrit scientifique, peut-être parce qu'elles ne savent pas très clairement elles-mêmes ce qu'elles veulent dire. De là un grave péril pour la langue anglaise. Je trouve que beaucoup d'écrivains, surtout aux Etats-Unis, et particulièrement ceux qui traitent des sciences sociales, ont maintenant un style tellement informe qu'il est impossible de prendre plaisir à la lecture de leurs ouvrages ou de les comprendre. Il faut veiller à ce que le même malheur n'arrive pas au français. La France a toujours montré au monde comment rendre, claires comme crystal, les pensées les plus subtiles et les plus nuancées. Je citerai l'exemple du mathématicien Henri Poincaré et du philosophe Henri

Bergson, qui ont su donner aux théories les plus complexes la grâce et la clarté d'oeuvres d'art.

Votre Association a un grand rôle à jouer. Elle doit favoriser la bonne littérature d'expression française au Canada, et conserver intactes les beautés de la langue. Bref, la même tâche vous est dévolue qu'à l'Académie française. Comme Anglais, Canadien d'adoption, ami depuis longtemps de la France et de sa tradition culturelle, je vous offre mes meilleurs voeux de succès.

THE INTEGRITY OF THOUGHT[1]

THE Association of Canadian Bookmen has for its chief purpose the extension of the reading habit among our people. Now there are habits and habits. A habit may be a dull automatic thing, with no zest in it and little meaning, a mere physical routine; or it may be the conscious ordering of our life for an intelligent purpose. It is the second which we seek to cultivate. If literature is to be a true formative force in our national life, then our readers must have the right attitude towards it. They must approach it with a keen enjoying temper, and with a proper edge to their mind. "We receive but what we give," said Coleridge, and unless we bring a good deal to books we shall take little away from them.

The first requisite is a mind in hard training—a mind with a just sense of values, with quick perceptions and with complete intellectual honesty. There is a gymnastic for the spirit as well as for the body. Very few of us give to our spiritual well-being the attention which we give to our physical health. We have far too much adipose tissue about us. Now the name we give to that spiritual adipose tissue is Cant, and our first duty is to obey Dr. Johnson's advice and "clear our minds of Cant."

Cant is not always easy to recognise, but it is easy enough to define it. It means mental and emotional insincerity. Intellectually it means the use of un-

[1] *Association of Canadian Bookmen. Montreal. 27th November, 1937.*

248

rationalised concepts out of laziness or a blind following
of fashion; a parrot-like use of vague counters of
thought which we have not really made our own.
Emotionally it means a parade of feelings which we do
not really possess. That is simple and will be generally
admitted. But note one thing. It is not the conscious
playing of a part. All of us at times have to dissemble—
to pretend to assent to something which we do not quite
understand, to simulate feelings which we do not
altogether share. Politicians and diplomats have constantly to make pretence in their professional duties.
Cant goes much deeper; when we are guilty of it we
have somehow battered ourselves into a belief that we
think or feel as we profess to think or feel, because the
edge of our mind has been blunted. It is what Plato
called "the lie in the soul"

I can best explain what I mean by taking instances,
and the most obvious are from public life. Politics are
conducted by a kind of shorthand. Creeds are telescoped into formulas and slogans and catchwords. That
is inevitable, for in the hustled business of public
controversy one must be content with summaries and
conclusions, and cannot always be expounding first
principles. The danger begins when we accept these
slogans without understanding what is behind them.
Government in a free country depends largely upon
intelligent discussion, and you cannot have intelligent
discussion if you deal only in empty counters, words
with no serious meaning behind them. We become like
the court jesters in the Middle Ages, and our weapons
are only bladders tied to sticks.

For example.—We habitually use the word "democracy" in our controversies, but how many of us have
ever considered what we mean by it? It is one of the

most difficult things in the world to define. Primarily, of course, it stands for a particular mechanism of government, the merit of which depends upon how it is handled. It denotes machinery not policy, function not purpose. A government, without ceasing to be democratic, can be tolerant or intolerant, bellicose or pacific, reactionary or progressive. But all of us are apt to read into it our own special ideals, and to defend a proposal because it is "democratic"—which is as if I were to defend the morality of a particular course of action on the ground that I undertook it voluntarily. We are all familiar with the circular argument that a thing is good for the people because it is democratic, and that it is democratic because it is good for the people. . . . So many other examples occur to me that it is hard to choose. But take the word "planning", a "planned economy". That has become truly a blessed word, a sure refuge for the muddled progressive. Of course there is a sound idea behind it. In the intricate and congested world of to-day we need more than ever foresight and close-textured thought in public affairs. We realise the defects of the *laissez-faire* creed of our fathers. But let us be chary of having recourse to planning as a panacea for all our ills. Let us realise that planning has as strict limitations as the old-fashioned method of go-as-you-please, that many things cannot be planned, that there must be unknown quantities which cannot be determined except in practice, that a rigid plan, without margin and without elasticity, is predestined to failure. . . . Lastly, I would deplore the way in which words like "fascism" and "communism" are slung about in political controversies. As they are frequently used to-day they are cant words, because in most cases there is no serious conception

behind them in the mind either of friends or opponents.
I agree with what the Prime Minister of Canada said
the other day, that the taunt of Fascist is used too
often to discredit some perfectly reasonable attempt to
maintain law and order, and the taunt of Communist to
discredit some rational scheme of social reform.

We can find many bad examples of cant in current
economics, and above all in religion. But let me rather
take the case of philosophy. A philosophical creed,
which is an interpretation of the universe, requires constant revision and restatement. A system devised by a
great thinker holds the ground for a generation, and
then it needs to be recast in the idiom of a changed
world. Moreover, gaps will appear in its structure and
certain aspects will be rightly queried. The system
does not perish, but its life depends upon its being perpetually criticised and examined, and thereby perpetually renewed. I may rightly call myself a Platonist
or an Aristotelian or a follower of Kant or of Hume
because I find in these thinkers the largest measure of
truth. But if I accept any system in its entirety and
rule out the need of criticism, then I am in danger of
cant, for I am a devotee of the letter and not of the
spirit. It becomes a dead scripture to me, not a living
thing, for I have shut it off from the free criticism which
is its breath of life.
Let me take a specific example from the great system
of idealism which is associated with the name of Hegel.
When I was a young man it was the fashionable
philosophic creed in Britain and America. Famous
teachers like Thomas Hill Green and Edward Caird,
and famous writers like F. H. Bradley and Bernard
Bosanquet had given it an almost classical standing.

But it was beginning to degenerate into a set of dogmas and formulas. It was fatally easy to give Hegelianism a theological colouring. It is said that in the philosophy paper in the final examination at Oxford, an irate examiner once set down as the first question, "Write down what you know of God, and don't mention Him in the rest of the paper". It was easy, too, to turn the doctrine into a set of *clichés*; a thing was only itself because it was also in some sense its opposite— contraries could always be reconciled in a higher unity,—and so forth. Hegelian idealism at the beginning of last century was in bad need of a spring cleaning.

Well, it got it. I pass over minor forms of dissent like Pragmatism and the philosophy of M. Bergson, and I would call attention to the work of Mr. Bertrand Russell and others in England, and the most interesting development of critical realism in America which, in its different forms, is identified with names like Dewey and Perry and Santayana. Hegelianism for the moment is at a discount. The present very vigorous philosophic impulse has a different orientation. But that does not mean that Hegelianism is dead. In our own day perhaps, and certainly in that of our children, new thinkers will arise to re-state it, for it contains an eternal core of truth. That is to say, it will live, but it will live only if it is constantly being re-examined and readjusted.

The philosopher to-day who is slavishly faithful to the old Hegelian terminology might, I think, justly be accused of cant, for he has shirked the critical revision which all creeds demand. I would point out to you what has always seemed to me to be a curious example of this shirking. Marxism is at the moment one of the most hotly debated of political creeds. I am not going to discuss its political aspect, though I might observe in passing that it would be a very good thing if people read *Das Kapital* before talking about it. Marxism has always claimed to have a philosophical background, and its exponents to-day love to enlarge upon the cosmic philosophy on which they base their practical creed. Now Marxism has for its base Hegelianism, as interpreted by those who are known in the history of philosophy as the "incomplete Hegelians", people like Feuerbach and Bruno Bauer. What interests me is that this philosophic background has been kept immune from criticism, and treated as a system of absolute truth which was beyond question. It is odd to find Marxians so full of iconoclastic zeal about historic and economic doctrines and the existing social fabric, and at the same time reposing smugly on a philosophic feather-bed, which has remained unchanged since the beginning of last century. They proudly appeal to what they call the dialectical method, apparently oblivious of the trenchant criticism of the Hegelian dialectic which has been going on for the last fifty years, criticism which no serious thinker can afford to neglect. Therefore I think we are entitled to say that on the philosophic side Marxism is guilty of cant.

I linger on this topic, for philosophy is a sphere where cant is specially easy and specially dangerous. It is comfortable to fall back, when in doubt, upon generalities, which have a sort of vague meaning for us and which are impressive to others. But it is cant none the less, and it is a proof of slackness and flabbiness of mind. Let us remember the pregnant philosophic metaphor, as old as Plato's *Theaetetus*. Our thoughts are like pigeons in a dove-cote. The pigeons in the dove-cote are in our keeping, and in a sense in our possession; but if we want to do anything with them, such as to make pigeon-pie, we must enter the dove-cote and get them actually into our hands. So with our thoughts; before they can be of real use and value they must cease to be generalities, which we only dimly appreciate, and become concrete and realised conceptions, with an organic place in our body of knowledge. "*Citius emergit scientia*", Francis Bacon wrote, "*ex errore quam ex confusione*"—"you will extract truth more readily out of actual concrete blunders than out of general confusion." Renan said the same thing, "*Malheur au vague; mieux vaut le faux*"—"A plague upon generalities! There is more value in honest error."

Let us get back to our proper subject, literature. If we are to read good books with a full understanding, and still more, if we attempt to produce literature ourselves, we must preserve a clean and fastidious palate. Our sense of values must be at once austere and catholic. We should be able to appreciate good writing of every kind—P. G. Wodehouse as well as Dean Inge, Professor Whitehead not less than James Thurber, "Colette" and Jean Cocteau equally with Jacques Maritain; but we should unhesitatingly reject whatever is crude or rancid or pretentious. We need this fastidiousness both for matter and style. In the first we demand what I have called the integrity of thought, and in the second we seek its equivalent, what Stevenson has called "the piety of speech". We must not let ourselves be beguiled by flashy heresies and transient fashions, for if we once permit our affections to stray to the third-rate or the fourth-rate we shall lose our power to appreciate the first-rate.

This attitude requires, as I have said, a keen enjoying mind with an edge on it, a loyalty to the highest standards. We must not be bemused by noisy heresies

and by the people who declare that the latest novelty
is the final word in wisdom. We must remember that
art is based on certain principles, or it ceases to be art.
The chief of these is that form and shape, what the
French call *ordonnance*, are essentials which cannot be
disregarded.

Let me give you an instance of what I mean. Some
thirty years ago a school of psychologists in Austria, of
whom Freud is the most famous, began the exploration
of the under-world of the soul, which they called the
subconscious. It was a most interesting and fruitful
line of enquiry, and it has produced results of enduring
value. I think one may fairly say that these psychologists tended to over-emphasize certain of their
discoveries, and, like every philosophic school, to fall
under the bondage of formulas, but no one can deny
the extreme importance of their best work. Un-
fortunately this new science became the fashion and
fell into the hands of the half-baked, and, as happens
in such cases, was very grossly misunderstood and mis-
applied. The unrationalised instincts, to which Freud
and his school drew attention, were given an undue
importance in the scheme of human life, and were used
as a key to unlock every riddle, a key which in most
cases did not begin to fit. Worse, the novelists got hold
of the thing and produced vast shapeless works which
were simply a rubbish-heap of stuff which they believed they had dug out of the subconscious. Now,
let me say frankly that I believe that Freud's discoveries are of high importance for the art of fiction.
You can see how a fine artist can handle them in the
delicate psychology of a writer like Virginia Woolf.
But the mere digging out and heaping up of material
from the subconscious has no value. It is not art, but
the raw stuff of art—*Ta pro tragodias*. It is crude ore

which has to be smelted and refined before it is precious metal. Unrationalised instincts must find a place in a rational scheme before they have any serious meaning for literature.

We should therefore demand shape and form, an integrated structure, both in the matter and the manner of literature. What must be the canon to guide us in this demand? There is only one—knowledge of the best books, the study of the greater minds. We must keep close to the classics—I do not mean the Latin and Greek only, but the classics of any tongues with which we are familiar. We may properly amuse ourselves now and then in the byways, but most of our journeying should be on the main highway which commands the noblest prospects and traverses the richest territory. You remember that phrase of St. Augustine which dominated Cardinal Newman's mind—"*Securus judicat orbis terrarum*", which we can translate in Shakespeare's words, "The great heart of the world is just", or in Gibbon's "the unerring sentence of Time". I wish someone would write a history of literary fads and heresies, merely to show how short-lived they are. In the past century in Britain we had the Dellacruscans in the beginning, and the Spasmodics in the 'fifties, and the Decadents in the 'nineties, and after the War we have had the dismal exponents of anarchic pessimism. Where are these coteries to-day? Dead as Queen Anne and scarcely remembered even by the historian. Time is the true winnower of wheat from chaff, and what remains from that winnowing is a possession for ever. So my last word to you this evening is that in our reading, while casting a generous net, we should hold close to the past, for in that past we have "titles manifold", we who speak the tongues of Shakespeare and Molière.